Data Warehousing 101

Data Warehousing 101

Concepts and Implementation

Arshad Khan

iUniverse, Inc.
New York Lincoln Shanghai

Data Warehousing 101
Concepts and Implementation

All Rights Reserved © 2003 by Arshad H Khan

iUniverse, Inc.

For information address:
iUniverse
2021 Pine Lake Road, Suite 100
Lincoln, NE 68512
www.iuniverse.com

Graphics are courtesy of Kirk A. Grothe, MPA, and Mark Alcasabas,
The Canton Group, LLC. www.cantongroup.com

ISBN: 0-595-29069-8

Printed in the United States of America

Contents

Terminology

- ❏ Aggregated data: Data obtained by combining data elements into a summarized format.
- ❏ Attribute: A data item containing information about a variable.
- ❏ Clickstream data: Data captured during the web browsing process.
- ❏ Data element: The fundamental data structure or most elementary unit of data in a data processing system.
- ❏ Data mapping: The process of matching (assigning) a source data element to a target data element.
- ❏ Metadata: Data about data such as data element or data type descriptions.
- ❏ Data mart: Small data warehouse that focuses on departmental needs, rather than the enterprise, which is typically limited to one or more specific subject areas.
- ❏ Drill-down: Method of analyzing detailed data that was used to create a summary level of data.
- ❏ Fact: Quantitative or factual data about a business.
- ❏ Measure: Numeric value stored in a fact table and in an OLAP cube, such as sales, cost, price and profit.
- ❏ Metadata: Data about data
- ❏ Redundancy: Storing multiple copies of the same data.
- ❏ Replication: Process of copying data from one environment to another while keeping data copies in sync with the source.
- ❏ Scalability: Ability to support larger data volumes and/or users.
- ❏ Scrubbing: Process for filtering, merging, decoding, and translating source data that ensures validated data populates the data warehouse.
- ❏ Slice and dice: A data analysis navigation technique; calls for interactive page. displays by specifying slices, or subsets of multi-dimensional arrays, via rotations and drill-down/up.

Introduction

Data Warehousing 101: Concepts and Implementation is an introductory book that addresses the needs of all those who are associated with data warehousing. It will be useful to those planning and implementing a data warehouse project, project managers, functional managers, business analysts, developers, power users, end-users, and project team members. *Data Warehousing 101: Concepts and Implementation* can be used as a textbook in an introductory data warehouse course. It can also be used as a supplemental text in IT courses that cover the subject of data warehousing.

Data Warehousing 101: Concepts and Implementation reviews the evolution of data warehousing and its growth drivers, process and architecture, data warehouse characteristics and design, data marts, multi-dimensionality, and OLAP. It also shows how to plan a data warehouse project as well as build and operate data warehouses. Also covered in depth are common failure causes and mistakes as well as practical guidelines and tips for avoiding common mistakes.

You should keep in mind that *Data Warehousing 101: Concepts and Implementation* is only an introduction to data warehousing, which encompasses many processes and technologies. Therefore, I encourage you to read other books to enlarge your knowledge of any topics touched on here.

Chapter 1

Understanding Decision Support Systems

DECISION MAKING AND EVOLUTION OF DSS
Understanding decision making

Decision making involves making a choice between alternative courses of action in order to achieve an objective or goal. For example, a decision maker facing lackluster sales, and studying options for increasing sales, may need to choose from among a number of alternatives. The potential alternatives might be to increase advertising, discontinue the worst performing products, change the distribution method and/or channels, etc. Decision making is usually geared towards managers who, primarily, are decision makers.

Range of decision making processes

Decision making can range from long-term strategic to short-term and tactical. The type of decision making required depends on the decision maker, whose objectives can be strategic or operational. The requirements of employees in the corporate hierarchy (such as the CEO, CFO, line manager and DSS analyst) are quite different. The reason is that the nature of the problems that they analyze can range from structured to unstructured processes.

Since the 1970s, there has been significant progress in the development of information processing systems, especially in areas where managers have had to struggle with complicated decisions. In response to their needs, there was an evolution of DSS systems whose objective was to help decision makers make difficult decisions.

What is a decision support system (DSS)

The term DSS has been redefined many times over the past couple of decades and, yet, there exists no universally accepted definition for it. One of the most applicable has been provided by Vidette Poe, "A DSS is a system that provides information to users so that they can analyze a situation and make decisions." Some of the other DSS definitions include:

❑ System that provides tools to managers to assist them in solving semi-structured and unstructured problems in their own, somewhat personalized way

❑ Model-based set of procedures for processing data and to assist a manager in his decision making

❑ Analytical technology that employs models for the solution of semi-structured and unstructured problems

❑ Computer-based system that helps the decision maker utilize data and models to solve unstructured problems

❑ Computer based information system that affects or is intended to affect how people make decisions

It must be understood that a decision support system is an adjunct to the decision maker. However, while it aids him and extends his capabilities, it does not replace his judgment.

Birth and evolution of decision support systems

During the early years of the computer age, managers worked off standardized, pre-defined, reports. Typically, such reports did not meet the needs of the lower-level decision makers. They also had a serious shortcoming in that they focused on reporting information to management—instead of supporting what it did with the information.

The term DSS was initially coined for the segment of information systems used to support complex decision making at a level that exceeded human ability to analyze complex issues and interrelated factors. They were geared towards applications that allowed managers to interactively query large databases and isolate information of interest pertaining to a specific problem.

The main business drivers of DSS over the years have been increased revenue, cost reduction, improved planning, increased control, and improved quality.

Application of decision support systems

Decision support systems can be applied wherever there is a requirement for decision support. Its use need not be restricted to specific functions or industries. Decision support systems can be applied in applications that are as diversified as workload and demand forecasting, operations planning and management, process evaluation and analysis, allocation of resources, etc. Implementation can be as diverse as optimizing the use of fuel and aircraft for an airline to taking market positions for a Wall Street firm.

COMPARISON AND BENEFITS
DSS characteristics and capabilities

There is no consensus regarding the definition of a DSS. Hence, there is no agreement regarding the characteristics and capabilities that should define a DSS. The following is a list of the common features that a decision support system is expected to have:

- ❑ Provide support for decision makers in semi-structured as well as unstructured situations through the interaction of humans with computer-based information
- ❑ Support that extends from top managers to line managers
- ❑ Supports individuals as well as groups
- ❑ Flexibility so that changes over time can be supported
- ❑ Supports decision making from concept to implementation
- ❑ Favors improvement in effectiveness over efficiency, i.e., accuracy, timeliness, and quality over cost
- ❑ Supports, rather than replaces, the decision maker; benefits from human experience and judgment while utilizing the speed and accuracy of computers
- ❑ Easy to use
- ❑ Need not involve high technology

Analytical versus operational systems

Operational systems are primarily used to run a company's business. They are transaction-based and support business application such as procurement, inventory, sales and order processing, accounting, human resources, etc. Such systems require fast access to the database, which is usually pre-defined. Decision support systems focus on analysis, including multi-dimensional view of the data, and the ability to run ad hoc reports. Such systems support drill-down and the requirement to slice and dice data. While the operational systems require performance, decision support systems need flexibility more than speed.

The characteristics of operational data and DSS data are also quite different. For example, the characteristics that define DSS data include high redundancy, flexible structure, large data volumes, analysis and management oriented, and ad hoc access. This is in contrast to operational data characteristics which include being detailed, transaction-driven, continuous updates, small data volumes, no redundancy, as well as high availability and reliability.

Decision support systems do not require a data warehouse

A decision support system does not mandate that its data source be a data warehouse, even though it is in many cases. Many companies use the data warehouse primarily for storing their historical data in one place, rather than as a source for their decision support systems. The most commonly used DSS tool is a spreadsheet. However, the ability of a corporate DSS system to access a data warehouse, that contains a goldmine of data, can make it even more useful than it would be by accessing less data in a smaller database.

Benefits of decision support systems

There are a number of benefits that can be attributed to decision support systems, which:

- ❑ Lead to objective decisions that can be defended
- ❑ Improve the efficiency and effectiveness of decision making
- ❑ Support the solution of complex problems
- ❑ Enable decision makers to better understand their business and industry
- ❑ Help managers focus more on analysis; can generate more alternative solutions to problems

- ❑ Enable simulation of various strategies, such as "what-if" analysis, quickly and objectively; consequences can be studied before implementation
- ❑ Enable thorough analysis in a short time frame
- ❑ Enable response to unexpected situations
- ❑ Improve management and control; actual performance can be compared against plans
- ❑ Improve performance
- ❑ Enable early discovery of problems
- ❑ Enable cost savings

Whom does it benefit

The traditional users of decision support systems were managers. However, with the introduction of user-friendly analysis tools and the explosive growth of data warehousing, the types of users has changed considerably in recent years. Currently, users range from top-level corporate managers to low-level workers. The most common users are business analysts and line managers. In many organizations, the decision making capability, due to the availability of easy-to-use DSS tools, has been lowered to clerical levels. For example, an inventory clerk can decide to reorder an item based on an analysis of goods movement into and out of the warehouse.

Chapter 2

Evolution of Data Warehousing

CONCEPTUAL BACKGROUND
Evolution of information processing requirements

The task of getting any meaningful data or information out of the early computer systems used to be very tedious. Consequently, a number of methods, techniques, and tools were developed to solve that problem. These included decentralized processing, extract processing, executive information systems (EIS), query tools, relational databases, etc. The need for timely and accurate decisions also led to the development of decision support systems.

Consequences of multiple applications and platforms

Traditional business applications were designed and developed with the objective of helping specific departments or functions such as marketing, human resources, finance, inventory management, loan processing, etc. Since such applications were typically developed independently and without coordination, over a period of time, they often contained redundant data. Also, the data residing in these applications was incompatible and inconsistent. Consequently, there was poor data management, enterprise view of data was lacking and, frequently, the same question would return different answers depending upon the application that was accessed. What made the situation even worse, especially after 1981 when the PC was introduced, was the explosion in the number of systems as well as the quantity and type of data being collected. The loss of a central data repository coincided with the widespread demand for timely and more information.

Limitations of transaction processing systems

Online transaction processing systems (OLTPs) were developed to capture and store business operations data. Since their main priority was to ensure robustness, rather than outputs or user accessibility, they suffered from some serious limitations. Their most obvious shortcomings were the inability to address the business users' need to access stored transaction data and management's decision support requirements. The OLTPs did not address history and summarization requirements or support integration needs—the ability to analyze data across different systems.

Another problem that has limited data extraction and analysis has been the limited availability of legacy systems' documentation that could be used effectively and efficiently. Even in modern systems, such as SAP which has more than 9,000 normalized tables, the available documentation leaves much to be desired and, consequently, data cannot be easily or quickly extracted by business users for their decision support requirements.

Birth of the data warehousing concept

The failure of the OLTP systems to provide decision support capabilities ultimately led to the concept of data warehousing in the late 1980s. Its objective, in contrast to OLTP systems, was to extract information instead of capturing and storing data and, hence, become a strategic tool for decision makers. Data warehousing aimed to become the foundation of corporate-wide DSS and business reporting that would support both tactical and strategic decision making.

In a way, the data warehouse concept involves a full circle. With the advent of the personal computer in 1981, islands of data had sprouted in an independence move away from the mainframe centralized concept. The data warehouse, by bringing together data stored in disparate systems, is a return to the centralized concept. The main difference is that data warehousing enables enterprise, and local, decision support needs to be met while allowing independent data islands to flourish.

DATA WAREHOUSING FUNDAMENTALS
What is a data warehouse

A data warehouse is a large analytical database which derives its data from a variety of production systems and is structured for querying, reporting, and analysis. The data warehouse, which can include both transaction as well as non-transaction data, is typically used as the foundation of a DSS that aims to meet the requirements of a large business user community. The data in a data warehouse can be accessed using a variety of front-end, easy-to-use, data-access tools.

Types of data warehouses
Enterprise data warehouse

An enterprise data warehouse contains data extracted from an organization's numerous systems that run its business. A typical company may have 5-10 systems that feed into its corporate data warehouse. Such a warehouse may contain detailed transaction as well as summarized data. The data, which is organized according to subjects such as sales or inventory, can range from a couple of years to 15 years. The period depends upon the requirements for analyzing historical trends across multiple business areas such as departments or regions. The amount of data stored in a data warehouse typically ranges in the gigabytes. However, many organizations now have data warehouses that contain terabytes of data.

Data mart

A data mart is a small data warehouse that contains a sub-set of the corporate data. Typically, its scope is limited to a department or business unit. A data mart, like a data warehouse, can include both detailed and summarized data. It is also fed from multiple systems though the number of its source data systems is far less compared to a data warehouse. The amount of data stored in a data mart is considerably less than in a data warehouse. Typically, a data mart will contain less than 100 GB of data.

Operational data store

An operational data store (ODS) is a subject-oriented database that contains structured data generated directly from transaction data sources. It contains very little or no summarized and historical data. An ODS is stored independently of the production system database(s). It contains current, or near current, data extracted from transaction systems. The objective of an ODS is to meet the ad hoc query, tactical day-to-day, needs of operational users. An ODS is often used as a staging area for data being imported into a data warehouse. In contrast to a data warehouse, which contains static data, an ODS can be frequently updated from operational systems—even in real-time.

Differences in operational and data warehouse data

An operational database primarily contains detailed transaction data that is collected from the organization's business operations. Though such a database may contain some derived data, which is calculated from the basic data elements, it primarily comprises of basic data elements. For example, the primary element can be the item price while the derived data can be the item's average price over a period of time. The data in an operational database is structured and organized in a manner that favors speed, performance, reliability, data integrity, and security.

A data warehouse also contains transaction data. However, it is also frequently populated with derived and summarized data. The availability of detailed data enables drill-down capabilities for those who want to dig deeper after they have analyzed the summarized data. For example, a manager can first analyze the sales performance of his sales force and, subsequently, selectively drill-down into the details of the under-performing salespeople.

Another key difference is that a data warehouse needs to deal with trends rather than data points. Therefore, its data elements need to have time associated with them, which is part of the key for every record in the database.

CONTRIBUTORS TO DATA WAREHOUSING EVOLUTION AND GROWTH

Data warehousing began to grow explosively starting in the mid-nineties. It is still characterized by high growth and, at this time, is considered to be a mainstream and strategic technology that a competitive organization cannot afford to ignore. There have been many reasons for the growth and acceptance of data warehousing, which are explained in the following sections.

Competitive environment

In the 1980s and 1990s, American corporations faced tremendous pressure to become more competitive and improve their productivity. As part of their effort to achieve a competitive edge, and become lean and mean, companies began to look more closely at the data that they collected over the years. Their need to analyze huge amounts of data, that was stored in disparate systems, and decision support requirements led to the explosion in data warehousing growth.

Globalization

The globalization of the world economy in the past two decades forced American companies to compete with foreign companies that could provide relatively low cost goods and services. Many American manufacturers could not compete in the new environment and, consequently, they had to be shut down or move their operations to Third World countries. The only way that American companies could compete in the new environment was by becoming more efficient and improving their productivity. To achieve their objectives, they made a serious attempt to use various technologies including data warehousing.

Economic factors

During the economic downturns that took place in the 1980s and 1990s, American companies downsized considerably and they made a serious effort to re-engineer their businesses. Continuous and never-ending changes in the environment forced management to become innovative and make the best use of their resources, humans as well as data, which contributed to data warehousing growth.

Key business drivers

The emergence of a number of key enabling technologies as well as many business drivers have fueled the growth of data warehousing. These key business drivers, which were driven by the need to compete more effectively in a very competitive environment, have been:

❑ Shorter product cycles that had lower tolerance for mistakes and slippages

❑ Need for increasing efficiency and productivity

❑ Growing demand for information at every level in the corporate hierarchy

❑ Need to support a strategy that enabled self-service for information access

❑ Need to leverage corporate data and its hidden value

Rapidly declining hardware prices

One of the most important factors in the growth of data warehouse deployment and use has been the sharp decline in the price of computer hardware, especially storage, even as there was a tremendous increase in computer processing power and capacity. Prices of processors, disk drives, memory, as well as peripherals have dropped dramatically in the past few years and, consequently, made data warehouse hardware more affordable.

Proliferation of data

The amount of data that is being collected has grown by leaps and bounds due to the desire of corporations to analyze as much data as they can. Major data proliferation contributors have been e-Commerce, e-Business, and the Internet. Terabyte data warehouses are quite common now and it is expected that the volume of data being captured will continue to grow.

More desktop power

The power of PC's today is far more than the mainframes of a few years ago. The PC has evolved from a personal productivity tool, that was initially used for word processing and simple spreadsheet calculations, to supporting sophisticated business applications and heavy-duty analytical analysis using multi-dimensional analysis tools. The development of PC capabilities has led to it being used as the primary tool for accessing data warehouses. Without the PC, the widespread use of data warehouses by end-users would not have been possible.

Technology developments: software and hardware

A number of technology developments have been the drivers of data warehousing growth. These include:

❑ Server operating software (Unix and Windows NT) characterized by:
  o Powerful features
  o Support for virtual memory, multi-tasking, and symmetrical multi-processing
  o Reliability
  o Easy and fast installation
  o Affordable cost

❑ Hardware developments including:
  o   Symmetric multi-processors (SMP)
  o   Massively parallel processors (MPP)
❑ Improvements in relational databases features and technology (RDBMS)
❑ Middleware development
❑ Widespread growth in networks
❑ Graphical user interface (GUI) tools

Growth in Internet and Intranets

The explosive growth of the Internet as well as Intranets, which are company networks based on the Internet standards, has also fueled data warehousing growth. The ability to access a data warehouse by those having a web browser, from any location, has eliminated the need to install or learn complex data access software and tools. Consequently, there are more users, with more varied requirements, who require access to information. Such users also create data as they browse the Internet or the Intranet.

Shift in focus from data to information

In the past, the focus had been on capturing and storing data. Therefore, management had to live with standard canned reports that, often, were not provided in a timely fashion. However, with changing corporate needs, that required quick decision making, management focus shifted from collecting and storing data to getting information out. When it was realized that the required information could not be extracted quickly or easily from the transaction systems, management began to explore various potential solutions including data warehousing.

Availability of application software

The widespread use of enterprise resource planning (ERP) software from SAP, PeopleSoft, Oracle, and others has led to the collection of huge amounts of transaction data. However, even though ERP software has been extremely good at collecting data, it has typically not been successful in satisfying the varied reporting needs of its users. Therefore, to meet their flexible reporting needs, many companies were forced to construct a data warehouse following an ERP implementation.

End-users are more technology savvy

The introduction of the personal computer has led to business users becoming more comfortable with computer technology. Their level of knowledge and sophistication has enabled them, across the corporate world, to become fairly independent of programmers and systems analysts for their analytical and reporting needs. Such users are able to use sophisticated software tools with minimum training. Additionally, there has also developed a large pool of technology-savvy business analysts who are as comfortable with technology as they are with business. Such users have been instrumental in making data warehouse projects succeed.

BENEFITS AND BENEFICIARIES
Benefits of data warehousing

The implementation of a data warehouse can provide many benefits to an organization. A data warehouse can:

- Facilitate integration in an environment characterized by un-integrated applications
- Integrate enterprise data across a variety of functions
- Integrate external as well as internal data
- Support strategic and long-term business planning
- Support day-to-day tactical decisions
- Enable insight into business trends and business opportunities
- Organize and store historical data needed for analysis
- Make available historical data, extending over many years, which enables trend analysis
- Provide more accurate and complete information
- Improve knowledge about the business
- Enable cost-effective decision making
- Enable organizations to understand their customers, and their needs, as well competitors
- Enhance customer service and satisfaction
- Provide competitive advantage
- Help generate new revenue (new customers), reduce costs (improved processes), and help the bottom line—profits

❑ Help expand the customer base

❑ Streamline business processes; can support DSS for various business processes such as manufacturing

❑ Provide easy access for end-users

❑ Provide timely access to corporate information

❑ Enable users to analyze data from different angles using powerful front-end access tools, which can drill-down as well as slice and dice

❑ Free users from dependency on IT as they can create their own reports quickly and independently

❑ Generate ROI of 100-400 percent in the first year for a well-designed data warehouse

Beneficiaries

The needs of these users can vary considerably because their information requirements and abilities can vary tremendously. For example, the different needs can be:

❑ Easy-to-use queries and reports, with few parameters, if the user is not technology savvy

❑ Ability to generate periodic reports for analyzing variances

❑ Ability to crunch numbers, slice and dice, and manipulate data and reports

When date warehousing technology was in its infancy, its primary users were decision making managers and business analysts, who did not have the technical knowledge to build reports from scratch. However, at this time, data warehouses are accessed by users across the enterprise, in practically every department, at all hierarchical levels including:

❑ Strategic users

❑ Operational users

❑ Managers

❑ Executives

❑ Novice and casual users

❑ Business analysts

❑ Power users

❑ Application developers

Chapter 3

Data Warehouse Characteristics and Design

BASIC CHARACTERISTICS

A date warehouse is characterized by four unique characteristics:

- ❑ Subject-oriented
- ❑ Integrated
- ❑ Time variant
- ❑ Non-volatile

Subject-oriented

Data warehouse data is organized by subjects such as customer, vendor, and products. This contrasts with classical applications that are organized by business functions such as loans, finance, inventory, etc. In a data warehouse, the major subject areas are physically implemented as a series of related database tables.

Integrated

The data in a data warehouse is always integrated—without any exception. Source data from multiple systems is consolidated in a data warehouse after undergoing various operations such as extraction, transformation, and loading. The data imported from the source systems reflects integration through consistent naming conventions, data attributes, measurement of variables, etc.

Time variant

Data warehouse data is accurate as of a moment in time while transactional data is accurate as of the moment of access. The data in a data warehouse consists of a lengthy series of snapshots, at various points in time, which can extend over a very lengthy period that can stretch 15-20 years. In contrast, typical operational databases contain data for only 6-24 months.

Non-volatile

The data stored in a data warehouse remains static. Any new data, which typically is introduced periodically, is appended. Data warehouse data is subjected to regular access and manipulation. However, activities such as insertion and deletion, which occur regularly with operational systems, do not take place in a data warehouse which is initially populated through a massive data load from the source systems followed by periodic appends.

DATABASE CHARACTERISTICS AND DESIGN
Comparing data warehouse and transaction databases

Data warehouse tables are extremely large. Such tables are highly interdependent and need to be periodically refreshed from multiple sources. Data warehouse data is historical and, therefore, time-dependent. It is primarily accessed on an ad hoc basis, rather than through a pre-defined method.

A transaction database that runs a business, also known as an OLTP system, is optimized for update functions—not for querying and analysis. It collects a large amount of raw transaction data which cannot be analyzed easily. Such a database does not address decision support requirements of history, summarization, integration, and metadata.

OLTP systems are not used as repositories of historical data, which is required to analyze trends. Typically, such systems have inconsistent, dynamic (changing rapidly), as well as duplicate and/or missing entries. Also, the data in transaction databases is not in a form that is meaningful to the end-user. The important characteristics of data warehouse databases and transactional databases are compared in the following table.

Data Warehouse	Traditional Database (OLTP)
Used for data retrieval and analysis	Used to run daily business transactions
Integrated data	Application specific data
Historical and descriptive data	Current, changing, and incomplete data
Organized by subject	Organized for performance
Non-volatile data	Updated data
Relational database structure	Relational database structure
Redundant data	Normalized data
Multi-dimensional data model	Normalized data model
Fewer but larger tables	Large number, but smaller, tables
Data for analyzing the business	Data for running the business
Summarized data	Raw data
Contains data about data (metadata)	Contains only data
Queries are unplanned and cannot be easily or quickly optimized	Queries are pre-defined, small, and can be optimized
Time element is contained in key structure	Time element may or may not be contained in key structure

Why data warehouse and transaction databases need to be different

The requirements of OLTP and data warehouse databases are quite different. While an OLTP database is geared to capture data quickly and efficiently for running the business, the objective of a data warehouse database is quite different—to retrieve and analyze the data. In contrast to an operational database, which needs to be updated continuously by the OLTP applications, a data warehouse database is updated periodically from the operational systems—typically during off-peak hours when network utilization is low. While OLTP databases require speed and performance, data warehouse databases are required to support heavy query volumes. Additionally, data warehouse and OLTP databases have different requirements for backup, recovery, transaction and data integrity, reliability, and availability.

Database design technique: Star schema

The star schema is the most widely-used method for implementing a multi-dimensional model in a relational database. It contains two types of tables, fact and dimension, which are described in detail Chapter 8. The schema takes its name from the star-like arrangement in which the fact table is surrounded by dimension tables. The star schema is not a normalized model, as its dimension tables are intentionally de-normalized, even though it is a relational model.

DATA DESIGN ISSUES
Normalization and de-normalization

An OLTP relational database is a collection of two-dimensional tables which are organized into rows and columns. In such a database, the design objective is to optimize table structures by eliminating all instances of data redundancy. This is achieved by making database tables as small as possible and, when required, merge selected tables through joins. Therefore, such a system contains a very large number of small tables in which there is minimum data redundancy.

In a data warehouse, the design objective is the opposite—to make database tables larger with more redundant data so that the need for table joins is minimized when a query is executed. If a query finds most of its required data in a single table, the need to access other tables is reduced. The technique of merging small tables into larger tables with data redundancy, called de-normalization, causes less input/output operations, which improves query performance. Therefore, since data warehouses are primarily used for querying and analysis, its tables are organized with a large degree of data redundancy.

De-normalization provides the flexibility for addressing requirements that are ad hoc and unplanned. However, while it is suitable for a data warehouse, it not appropriate for a transaction database which emphasizes performance over redundancy. A normalized transaction database limits the queries that can be run against it due to performance issues.

Database partitioning

The objective of partitioning is to break up data into smaller physical units that can be managed independently. This technique provides more flexibility in data management for designers and operations personnel. It overcomes the limitations of large physical units which cannot be easily structured, reorganized, recovered or monitored. Partitioning enables sequential scanning, if required, as well as ease of indexing. It allows data to be broken up by region, organization, business unit, date, etc., which can be very useful for the purpose of analysis.

Aggregation

To improve the performance of queries, data can be aggregated or accumulated along pre-defined attributes. For example, car sales data can be aggregated by geography and model by adding the sales dollars for each model within a specific geography. Similarly, overall sales can be added up for a week, month, quarter or year. Hence, when a query is run against aggregated data, the response is faster as less data needs to be accessed (since the data is already aggregated). The data to be stored in an aggregated format is determined by a number of factors including the frequency of queries.

Levels of data

Data is stored in data warehouses at three levels:

❑ Current detailed data: such as transaction level data

❑ Lightly summarized data: such as revenues by week or by sub-region

❑ Highly summarized data: such as revenues by month or by region

Each data level is targeted to a different type of user ranging from senior executives to operational users. While an inventory clerk may monitor the inventory of specific items at the detailed level, the chief executive may be more interested in analyzing highly summarized data that can provide insight into the performance of the various regions, business units, subsidiaries, product lines, etc.

Current detailed data

The bulk of a warehouse consists of current detailed data, at the lowest level of granularity (detail), which is extracted from the operational systems. It is organized by subject area and can be stored as raw or aggregated data. All data items at this level represent snapshots in time. The period for which current detailed data is maintained in a data warehouse varies from organization to organization. Typically, data for five years is maintained though many companies store data for 10-15 years. The frequency of data refresh also varies according to organizational needs. Many companies perform a daily data load, while some prefer to refresh the data in real-time.

Lightly summarized data

The requirement for light data summarization in a data warehouse is based upon the fact that most users run queries that repeatedly access and analyze the same data elements at a summarized level. Therefore, by providing summarized data, there can be considerable improvement in ease of access, performance, and storage requirements.

Highly summarized data

The source for the highly summarized data can be lightly summarized data or current detailed data. The primary users of highly summarized data are senior executives and strategic users. While their needs are primarily limited to this level, they can also access lower level detailed data through a drill-down process.

Data archiving

The data to be archived, and its frequency, depends on how the data is used. If the data warehouse supports operational needs, retaining two years of data may be sufficient. However, if the data is being analyzed for strategic purposes, the retention requirements may extend for a considerably longer period, which may be 5-15 years. The archived data granularity may be the same as the current detailed or aggregated data.

Granularity

An important data warehouse design issue is the level of detail, or granularity, to be maintained for the data because it affects the volume of data to be stored and the type of query that can be executed. If data is highly granular, with a very high level of detail, the amount of data to be stored in the warehouse will be huge. A highly granular warehouse contains very detailed data, which can extend to every captured transaction, such as an individual sales order or a purchase requisition. A less granular warehouse contains a higher level of data such as total purchase orders issued for each month or total monthly sales by region.

If the stored data is very granular, practically any type of query can be run against it. However, if the data is less granular, the types of queries that can be run against it will be limited. Usually, senior executives and decision makers require summarized and aggregated data, while operational staff require detailed data. However, this distinction is being blurred as the needs and requirements of these two types of users have overlapped, due to changes in the decision making levels and approaches, in recent years.

DATA MODELING
Data models

Database design is accomplished in five steps: planning and analysis, conceptual design, logical design, physical design, and implementation. The objective of data modeling is to develop an accurate model or graphical representation of the business processes, the data that needs to be captured in the database, and the relationships between data. A data model, which is created in the conceptual design step, focuses on the data required and its organization—rather than the operations to be performed on the data. It represents data from the users' perspective and is independent of hardware and software constraints. A widely used methodology for creating a data model is the Entity-Relationship model, which is expressed as an Entity-Relationship Diagram (ERD). The most widely used model for capturing data warehouse requirements is the dimensional model, which is also known as the star schema.

Logical data model

A logical data model graphically depicts the information requirements of a business. It combines the business requirements and data structure—the two most important components of application development. If either one of these is lacking or poorly defined, the result will be an application that fails or is not well-accepted.

A logical data model is independent of a physical data storage device. While a logical database describes the business requirements, the physical database indicates how they are implemented. A logical data model uses an ERD to put together all the data items or information required to run a business. It includes relationships, cardinality, attributes, and keys. An ERD is created by a data modeler based upon the requirements specified by the business experts.

Physical data model

The physical data model is created from the logical data model. Based on the physical data model, the physical database is designed and implemented. The activities in this step include de-normalizing the data, selecting keys, creating indexes, building referential integrity, etc. A well designed physical data model and database structure ensures system performance and ease of maintenance.

Importance of building a data model

It is imperative that a logical data model be built for every data warehouse project even though it is a very labor-intensive and time consuming activity. A logical data model is the foundation upon which a database for an application is designed. It verifies that the system will satisfy the business needs. The implementation approach and technique is determined to a large extent by the business requirements and the logical data model.

A data model ensures that the data required by the database is represented accurately, completely, and is in a format that can be reviewed by end-users before the design is implemented. The data model is used to build the physical database as it contains information for defining the tables, keys, triggers, and stored procedures. Without a data model, database design will be seriously flawed, efficiency and performance will suffer and be less than optimal, data for critical reports may be missed, results produced may be inconsistent, maintenance will be difficult, and supporting the business needs will not be easy.

Chapter 4

Process and Architecture

PROCESS
Data warehouse process components

A data warehouse is an integrated process, shown in Figure 1, that encompasses many technologies. The basic process involves moving data from various databases into a central database, called a data warehouse, where it is stored and subsequently analyzed. The data is moved using a variety of acquisition techniques and tools.

A data warehouse consists of many components, ranging from simple to complex, which can be grouped into three main categories:

❑ Acquisition component: interfaces with the source systems and is used for importing data into the data warehouse

❑ Storage component: is a large physical database used for storing data imported into the data warehouse

❑ Access component: is used to access and analyze data stored in the data warehouse; consists of front-end access and query tools

Figure 1
Data Warehouse Architecture

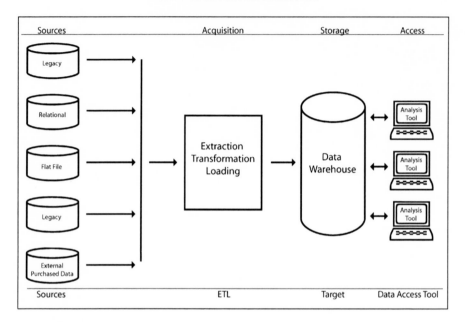

Acquisition component

The data fed into a data warehouse can originate from many sources though, typically, it is imported from the organization's transaction database(s). The sources can be mainframe files, relational and non-relational databases, flat files, etc. Many companies also use external sources to feed data into their data warehouse. Most of these sources cannot meet the data warehouse requirement for its data to be in a specific format (layout) which supports query processing. The reason for this shortcoming is that most data sources are formatted for transaction processing—not analysis.

The source data, before it can be loaded into the data warehouse, typically needs to undergo major formatting and transformation whose aim is to remove inconsistencies and achieve standardization. For example, gender in three source systems may be coded differently: M/F, male/female, and 1/2. Before such data can be exported to a data warehouse, at least two must be transformed so that all three source systems feed data into the warehouse in the same format.

All source data may need to undergo some or all of the following operations in the data warehousing process:

- Mapping (from source databases to target database)
- Cleaning dirty data (for missing, incorrect, or inconsistent data within fields)
- Restructuring and reformatting, which can be due to field lengths, sequence, data types (text, numeric, alpha-numeric)
- Recalculation
- Selection (using filters such as if/then)
- Summarization
- Validation
- Reconciliation (when data is imported from multiple sources)

The overall data acquisition process, called ETL (extraction, transformation, and loading), is generally grouped into three main components:

- Extraction: Involves obtaining the required data from the various sources.
- Transformation: Source data undergoes a number of operations that prepare it for import into the data warehouse (target database). To perform this task, integration and transformation programs are used which can reformat, recalculate, modify structure and data elements, and add time elements. They can also perform calculations, summarization, de-normalization, etc.
- Loading: Involves physically placing extracted and transformed data in the target database. The initial loading involves a massive data import into the data warehouse. Subsequently, an extraction procedure periodically loads fresh data based on business rules and a pre-determined frequency.

The ETL task, which is very complex, is at the heart of the data warehousing process. It can include tasks such as:

- Merge processing when multiple data sources are used
- Purge processing when some filtering rules are applied to weed out unwanted data
- Staging when source data needs to be placed in an intermediate storage location before it is read by, and imported into, the data warehouse
- Back flushing if the clean data warehouse data is to be sent back to the legacy (source) system(s)

The ETL tasks are handled by a variety of tools. Some of them, such as file transfer programs, are fairly simple. However, some tools, such as those used for data transformation, can be fairly complex. They can automate data extraction from multiple sources, map sources to the target database, transform and/or manipulate data, and load data into the data warehouse.

Storage component

There are two databases associated with a data warehouse. They are:

❑ Source database

❑ Target database

Source database

This database feeds data into the data warehouse. In a typical organization, there are multiple data sources of different types, such as relational and hierarchical, and sizes. In the overwhelming majority of cases, the source database contains current operational data. However, in some cases, the source is a non-transactional database, such as a data warehouse or a data mart, which contains data stored in de-normalized tables. Examples of source data, which can be extracted from internal as well as external sources, include:

❑ Internal systems: financial, billing, materials management, sales, manufacturing, etc.

❑ External data: industry, economic, demographic, weather, clickstream, etc.

Target database

The core component of a data warehouse system is a very large target database. It holds the organization's transaction and historical data in an integrated format. Due to its analytical and query processing requirements, data warehouse data is structured in a de-normalized format in contrast to the normalized format of transaction databases. The size of a data warehouse can be huge. For example, the Home Depot data warehouse, which was commissioned in 2002, has been designed for 60 terabytes of storage.

While conceptually, only two databases are required (source and target) for a data warehouse, a third type of database is also used frequently. This is an intermediate database, an operational data store, into which source data is loaded and stored before being sent to its final destination—the data warehouse.

Access component

To access and analyze the data stored in a data warehouse, and present it to the users, an access/query component is required—which can include query, reporting, and decision support tools. Such tools, which can include data mining software, can typically support queries, calculations, what-if analysis, as well as other functions.

Most data warehouse users use standard reports and queries. They run most of their queries using summary views. Only a small percentage of data warehouse users create custom reports, which are often created by business analysts.

The sophistication of the data access tools varies significantly. They range from low-end tools, with simple querying capabilities, to high-end tools that can perform sophisticated multi-dimensional analysis. The recent trend has been to web-enable such tools, a feature that provides many benefits. It makes the tool more versatile and easy to use, eliminates the need to install special software on every desktop, provides access through a simple browser, and reduces cost due to the requirement for less powerful and expensive hardware.

ARCHITECTURE
Metadata

Metadata, or data about data, is a key element in the data warehouse architecture. Just as a library's card catalog helps locate books, metadata provides useful information for locating data stored in a data warehouse. All data about the data, as mapped between the source and target systems, is resident in the metadata. The metadata includes a description of the data warehouse fields and tables, data types, and acceptable value ranges.

The metadata can help determine mapping information, such as where the data warehouse data came from—legacy systems, files, databases, and fields. It provides information about the data structure—tables and columns as well as their definition and descriptions. Additionally, metadata indicates the relationships between the data structures within or between databases. It also provides information about operations performed on imported data such as:

❏ Selection criteria and business rules that were applied
❏ Transformation and integration performed during the data migration process
❏ Filtering and cleansing that was performed
❏ Algorithms used to summarize and derive data

Metadata is often resident outside the data warehouse, in a database or a formal repository, and used to track the relationship between the data model and the data warehouse. It can provide information on how the business definitions and calculations changed over the years. Metadata can also provide a history of extracts and changes in data over time.

There are two types of metadata: structural and access. Structural metadata is used to create and maintain the data warehouse. Its foundation is the data warehouse model that describes data entities as well as their relationships. On the other hand, access metadata provides the dynamic link between a data warehouse and its associated applications.

Physical architecture and infrastructure

A data warehouse system consists of several physical components that are connected through a network structure, which glues the parts together. The system hardware consists of the acquisition, storage, and access components. The deployment is typically implemented in a 2-tier or 3-tier architecture, or physical configuration, as described in the next section.

Other components that make up the data warehousing system include the operating system, system utilities, procedures, and middleware connectivity tools. The middleware links different data sources to the data warehouse and provides connectivity between the data warehouse and associated clients.

Data warehouse usage grows exponentially if it is implemented successfully. However, success can create capacity constraints if the system and network are inadequately designed. Hence, it is important that the data warehouse be designed so that it is scalable, can accommodate growth, exhibits good performance and avoids slow response times.

Application and deployment architecture

The data warehouse application architecture comprises of the three components, or layers, that make up an application. They are:

❏ Presentation (what the user sees—the client side view)

❏ Functional logic (underlying business rules)

❏ Data (physical data storage layer)

The simplest deployment is a two-tier architecture where a client, such as a PC, interacts directly with a server. In a two-tier system, the first tier (server) hosts the data warehouse database. The client, the second tier, hosts the front-end decision support and analysis tools. The three-tier architecture is more complex as it introduces an intermediate tier between the server and the client. It has the following components:

- ❑ 1st tier: server tier which handles data processing
- ❑ 2nd tier: application tier that supports the functional logic and services
- ❑ 3rd tier: client or desktop tier which handles the decision support and presentation component

Defining the architecture

An approach that works quite well, in most cases, is to have a flexible architecture which supports the implementation of best-of-breed tools over time and allows the easy replacement of individual components. The architecture should meet the current needs as well as future requirements—when the data warehouse is expanded or upgraded.

A data warehouse should not be designed for a particular technology. Its architecture must be designed before the technology is selected. Failure to design the architecture first can lead to the requirements not being supported by the selected technology, which cannot be easily changed or discarded due to the extremely high costs associated with dumping or changing a deployed infrastructure. Since many options are available, as many technologies support data warehousing, rarely should an overriding factor force a company to implement a particular technology for its data warehousing needs.

Chapter 5

Data Migration

NEED FOR DATA MIGRATION

The data to be analyzed in a data warehouse needs to be imported from a company's legacy, operational, databases. The migration task is very complicated as the number, type, and quality of the sources feeding the data warehouse can vary significantly. The migration effort requires considerable effort because the source data and processes need to be thoroughly analyzed. In many implementations, 75% of the time required to build a data warehouse is spent on the following tasks:

❑ Extracting data from the sources

❑ Conditioning and transforming source data for meeting the data warehouse requirements (technical and business)

❑ Loading the data into the data warehouse

Many software tools can be used to automate data migration to a considerable extent. Despite that, the data migration task still requires considerable manual effort, which can be a significant part of the total effort expended for the overall project, especially if custom ETL programs are used.

Data quality requirements

The quality of information provided to users is a critical data warehousing success factor as it has the potential to directly impact the company's profitability. The data warehouse is a gold mine that contains the corporate strategic data, which can be used by decision makers at all hierarchy levels. If the

30

data is inaccurate and unreliable, the data warehouse will lose its credibility and, consequently, be ignored by the users. If inaccurate data is used for decision making, the quality of decisions will be seriously compromised and severe consequences can be expected. Hence, data warehouse data must be accurate and meet the highest quality standards with the following characteristics:

❑ Clean

❑ Consistent

❑ Accurate

❑ Complete

❑ Reliable

❑ Relevant and useful

❑ Understandable

❑ Current

❑ Timely

Concrete steps need to be taken to ensure data quality. The data cleanup process must start at the source data, which often requires complex cleaning. The data imported into the data warehouse must be checked and validated to ensure that it is properly structured, accurate, and complete. Failure to do so can have serious repercussions including project failure.

Problems with source data

Source data imported into a data warehouse is often dirty and inconsistent. For example, a vendor loaded into the data warehouse from three different sources may be referred to as IBM, International Business Machines, and IBM Global Services. Consequently, any analysis or summation run on a data warehouse which contains these three variations will not return accurate results.

The range of problems commonly encountered cover a wide spectrum. For example, field data does not match the field description, data files from various sources have different formats, name is spelled differently in different systems, address varies across sources, multiple names are located in the same field, name and address are in the same field, special characters are used inconsistently, addresses have missing zip codes, phone numbers have missing area codes, spacing is inconsistent, data is truncated, etc. Hence, an important task that needs to be performed at each data warehouse project is to check and validate the data being imported.

DATA MIGRATION STEPS
Identifying data sources

The initial step in the data migration process is to identify the operational sources that will feed data into the data warehouse. Duplication is a common problem and many data elements can be found in multiple data sources. Therefore, the most appropriate source for feeding the data warehouse must be identified in this task. Such a source and its data elements must be reliable and accurate. They must preferably be in the required format or need minimum transformation for import into the data warehouse. To perform the data identification task, considerable time and effort is usually required due to the differences and possible anomalies among the various source databases.

Data cleansing

Before source data is acquired and loaded into the target database, it is cleansed in order to remove errors that are commonly found in the source systems. This task can involve a number of steps such as identifying redundant data, rectifying erroneous values in fields, populating fields with missing values, standardizing the format, etc. There is a direct relationship between the amount of effort expended in data cleansing and the number of loading errors encountered when data is moved from the source to the target database. In general, greater the amount of data cleansing effort, lower is the number of expected errors.

Acquisition

After the data to be imported into a data warehouse has been identified, it is physically acquired from the source databases. In this step, called data acquisition, data is extracted from the source(s) and transported to the target database, However, before the data is transported and loaded into the target, it is subjected to some transformations which change its characteristics. The transformations can include restructuring the data, de-normalizing the tables, adding new fields and keys, etc. Before loading, the data can also be subjected to various operations such as consolidation (merging various data sets into a single master data set), standardization (of data types and fields), scrubbing (cleaning to remove inconsistencies or inaccuracies), summarization, etc.

A number of tools can be used for the transformation process. Such tools need to be powerful, easy to use, and flexible so that they can be used in a broad range of applications.

Loading

The data from the various sources is initially fed into a data warehouse in a massive upload. Subsequently, new data is introduced with a frequency ranging from a few days to real-time, depending on the organization's requirements. Another type of upload is in the reverse direction. In such a case, the data warehouse data is fed back to its source—which can be a legacy system, another data warehouse, or a data mart.

DATA MIGRATION CHALLENGES
Legacy source data issues

Data warehouses are fed data from legacy systems, which are characterized by many serious issues that can be quite challenging. The common issues include:

❑ Accuracy: Typically, legacy systems' data quality is quite poor which, if not corrected, can translate into serious problems such as flawed analysis and, consequently, incorrect decisions

❑ Formatting: Files extracted from multiple sources, for migration to a data warehouse, will usually have data stored in different formats

❑ Field descriptions do not match the data values or follow business rules

❑ Granularity of data in the source databases can vary considerably

❑ Mapping may not be simple or straightforward as the data structure and storage format can vary considerably across systems

❑ Difficult to match and relate entities, which can be a roadblock for a consolidated view—such as subsidiaries under a single organization; such data may need to be rebuilt

❑ Business entities may be represented in many ways, which makes matching and consolidation a complex task; hence, ensuring entity integrity becomes a requirement

Data preparation

The task of populating a data warehouse with data from multiple sources is a very challenging task that requires a large investment of time and resources. It has to be performed in an environment characterized by multiple data sources, varying data quality, inconsistent nomenclature and definitions, inconsistent data, data models that vary across the enterprise databases, consolidation requirements across non-standard aging legacy systems, lack of skilled legacy IT resources, etc. These challenges and risks can be mitigated to some extent by the available state-of-the art tools for data transformation, cleansing, capture, and loading.

Automating data migration

The initial data load into a data warehouse is very large. Even though data marts are smaller, their initial data load volumes can be fairly significant. Subsequently, new data needs to be introduced, periodically, to refresh and update the data warehouse. For this purpose, pre-defined extraction, mapping, and loading routines are used to feed data from the operational systems at pre-defined frequencies. As required, such routines can be automated to extract source data and move it to the data warehouse, while maintaining data integrity during the transfer, based on pre-defined business rules.

Selecting the tools

Many tools are available to perform data migration tasks. The products, which are quite versatile, have functions such as validating names and addresses when multiple sources are being consolidated, rectifying errors in the data elements, creating new data in the format required by the data warehouse, etc. The challenge is to select an appropriate tool that can meet the conflicting requirements of ease of use, data quality requirements, speed, scalability, cost, application requirements, and future usage.

Chapter 6

Infrastructure, Tools, and Vendor Selection

INFRASTRUCTURE

Hardware

A data warehouse system consists of a number of hardware components such as servers, workstations (PCs), memory, disk storage units, networks, etc. The selection of the hardware platform and components depends on a number of factors including:

❑ Storage capacity

❑ Scalability

❑ Performance

❑ Number of users

❑ Operating system

❑ Software

❑ Complexity of queries

❑ IT skills and maintenance capabilities

Data warehouse usage increases dramatically if users perceive it to be useful. However, past experience has shown that the rapid rise in the number of users usually surprises designers. The underestimation of usage and, consequently, hardware requirements creates problems when the number of users increase beyond expectations and queries start to become more complex.

Data warehouse engine

Engine requirements

A data warehouse engine, the database, provides the structure for storing the data required to support the analysis requirements. Some of the engine's primary business requirements, and factors that determine its selection, include:

- ❑ Ease of use
- ❑ Flexibility
- ❑ Scalability
- ❑ Reliability
- ❑ Performance
- ❑ Data loading time
- ❑ Ability to support expected data volumes
- ❑ Ease of monitoring and administration
- ❑ Ability to work with various access tools from different vendors
- ❑ Security
- ❑ Vendor (reputation and number of database installations)

Type of database to use

A key data warehouse design decision concerns the database type to be selected: relational database or multi-dimensional (OLAP) database. The characteristics of these database types, and their differences, are explained in detail in Chapter 9. The selection of the database type significantly influences the choice of the data access tool which can be a simple relational query tool, ROLAP tool that provides a multi-dimensional view of the data, or some other type of specialized decision support tool.

Each database type is characterized by strengths and limitations. Conventional relational databases support the specialized technical requirements of data warehouses such as data extraction and replication, query optimization, bit-mapped indexes, etc. However, they provide limited support for data cleanup and transformation functions. The strengths of multi-dimensional databases include the benefits associated with OLAP as well as fast querying and performance. However, their important drawback is that they are based on a proprietary database solution.

Conventional relational databases provide many of the features that character-ize multi-dimensional databases. In many cases, either type of database can be used. However, for specialized or complex analysis requirements, multi-dimensional databases are often preferred. In general, wherever possible, con-ventional relational databases should be used. A proprietary tool, such as a multi-dimensional database, should be used only if there is clear justification for its use.

DATA MIGRATION TOOLS
Role and importance of ETL

An extremely important and difficult task in building a data warehouse is extracting, transforming, and loading a huge amount of data that is stored in a variety of disparate legacy systems. The ETL design and development task is also very expensive and can easily consume 50-75% of the data warehouse project cost. The task is very time consuming because it requires cleaning and integrating the organization's data, which is stored in many systems and for-mats, so that it can be used easily and effectively. Hence, it is critical that ETL be accomplished through a well-designed architecture that is reliable and scal-able. Such an architecture must support the extraction, transformation, and loading of the data elements that need to be fed into the data warehouse.

ETL tools can be very expensive and difficult to use. They have the potential to cause serious problems including project failure and, hence, should be selected very carefully based on the unique needs of each data warehouse.

ETL tasks

Many tools, from a number of vendors, are available for building a data ware-house. The three primary functions that ETL tools, which move data from one location to another, are required to accomplish are:

- ❑ Read data from a source such as a relational database table, flat file, etc.
- ❑ Manipulate data (filter, modify or enhance) based on specific rules
- ❑ Write resulting data to the target database

Specific tasks that an ETL tool may have to perform range from:

❑ Converting data: changing the incoming source data into a unified format and definition

❑ Deriving data: applying mathematical formula to field(s) in order to create a brand new field

❑ Filtering data: screening unwanted data from source data files before being moved to the data warehouse

❑ Integrating data: merging files from different databases and platforms

❑ Summarizing data: combining tables

❑ Selecting data: selecting and loading data based on triggers

ETL tools

The functionality of the available ETL tools varies considerably and their cost can range from minimal to hundreds of thousands of dollars. At the lower end are simple data migration tools whose functionality is limited to extraction and loading. However, the more versatile tools are very sophisticated and can perform many tasks such as enabling transformation, handling a wide range of input formats and sources, etc.

As users clamor for complete solutions, vendors are being forced to provide more functionality and reliability. Some of the desired features include:

❑ Back-end data management and processing including metadata management

❑ Ability to handle real-time, or near real-time, data as batch processing windows become smaller and smaller

❑ Ability to handle greater number of sources and different data sources (XML, HTML, etc.)

❑ Improved administration

❑ Ability to handle greater complexity of mappings and transformations

❑ Improved throughput and scalability for handling rising data volumes even as batch processing windows decrease

❑ Improved capability for capturing changes and updates

❑ Ease of use for loading and/or updating

DATA ACCESS AND MINING TOOLS
Need for data access

Transaction processing systems have been very effective in capturing and storing operational data. However, historically, they have lacked the ability to effectively utilize the stored data and convert it into information that can be used for decision support. Therefore, in recent years, this limitation has led to the development and popularity of tools, such as data warehouses, that enable users to access stored data and transform it into information.

Requirements

The data access and reporting requirements within an organization vary considerably. At the high end are the strategic queries that analyze huge amounts of data across multiple dimensions. At the low end are the tactical queries, run against limited data which may be frequently updated, that answer operational questions. The requirements of strategic users, the senior executives, are quite different compared to line managers, front-line workers, and power users. Their requirements can range from canned status reports, which are most widely used, to ad hoc queries that are developed dynamically and interactively.

The challenge is to create a reporting environment where the needs of all users can be met. This requires balancing the needs of the vast majority of non-technical users, whose needs fall within limited parameters, to the requirements of some users who demand performance and flexibility. The deployment of such a reporting environment, which must be scalable and secure within a controlled environment, must meet the varying needs of business users and avoid straining IT resources. If the reporting tools are not used to their expected potential by the users, which can be caused by a number of reasons, the data warehouse will end up being viewed as a limited success or a failure.

Data access tools
Features

Some of the basic requirements of data access products include flexibility to meet the diverse needs of users having a wide range of requirements, scalability, low implementation cost, fast implementation, web access, support for different output types, extensive formatting capabilities, adaptability to changing business needs, ease of use and administration, security, etc.

Categories

The commonly used data access products fall into the following main groups:

❑ Query and reporting tools, which can be deployed cost-effectively for a large number of users. These tools, which have extensive formatting capabilities, cannot answer complex questions that require drill-down capabilities

❑ Spreadsheets such as Excel

❑ DSS tools that can perform multi-dimensional analysis against relational database systems

❑ Tools that can access multi-dimensional databases

❑ Data mining products

❑ Tools, such as SAS and SPSS, that can perform complex statistical analysis

❑ Artificial intelligence and advanced analysis tools

Multi-dimensional analysis

A number of multi-dimensional OLAP tools, from different vendors, are available for analyzing data warehouse data. The features and benefits of this technology, which has powerful navigation and presentation capabilities, are described in Chapter 9.

Data mining

Data mining is a sophisticated technique that analyzes large volumes of data, for determining patterns and relations, using advanced statistical analysis and modeling techniques. Conceptually, it aims to generate a hypothesis. The objective is to find patterns that can be leveraged for improving the business. For example, a credit card company may like to analyze its data for identifying potential defaulters or a phone company might like to identify churners—those who are likely to switch carriers.

Data mining is based upon a number of algorithms. These include neural networks, induction, association, fuzzy logic, and visualization. The more the number of algorithms used, greater is the probability of finding some pattern. Data mining can unveil strange but useful associations. For example, a retailer discovered that almost half of the customers who bought diapers on Friday also bought beer—an association that led the retailer to display the two products side by side. Retailers can mine data to an extent where they can determine which products were bought together, the path the customer followed through the store and, consequently, determine the most effective sales floor layout.

The heaviest users of data mining, a technique that is still in its infancy, are retailers and telecommunication companies. Data mining is widely used in banking, insurance, health care, and transportation industries. Some of its applications include:

- ❑ Identifying buying patterns
- ❑ Predicting responses to advertising
- ❑ Uncovering credit card usage and fraud
- ❑ Identifying behavior of risky or fraudulent customers
- ❑ Customer retention
- ❑ Identifying potential new customers
- ❑ Product failure analysis
- ❑ New business opportunities

In contrast to OLAP, which answers specific questions, data mining can discover patterns. For example, while OLAP can provide the average transaction size for credit cards, stolen versus non-stolen, data mining can help uncover buying patterns associated with the fraudulent use of credit cards.

VENDOR SELECTION
Selection approaches

The choice of the wrong tool, component or vendor can create many problems and, in the worst case, even derail a data warehouse project. A vendor should be selected with extreme care after an evaluation of the pros and cons of the following two approaches:

- ❑ Best of breed: best product is chosen, for each category or component, and then integrated
- ❑ Turnkey project: vendor provides all the major components required for creating the data warehouse—from ETL through end-user access

Choice of vendors

In the first few years after the introduction of data warehousing, each process area was catered to by a few vendors who specialized in that area. However, as data warehouse technology started to become mainstream, the larger vendors started to offer products in most areas—either through in-house development or by acquiring niche players. At this time, there are many vendors who provide a complete suite of data warehousing products and services.

The Appendix lists the leading vendors who provide the wide range of components and tools that are required to design, implement, and operate data warehouses and data marts.

Chapter 7

Data Marts

CHARACTERISTICS AND BENEFITS
Data warehouse limitations and data mart drivers

Data warehouses have provided many benefits that organizations have leveraged to their competitive advantage. However, they have also been characterized by some limitations, which have forced companies to seek alternative solutions for their information needs, including the following:

❑ Lag between need and implementation: It used to take a very long time, sometimes years, from the time a data warehouse was requested till the time it was actually rolled out to the users.

❑ Huge size and scope of data warehouse projects encompassing the entire organization. Such projects used to be very expensive—costing millions. They also spanned a very lengthy period and, in some cases, took years to implement.

❑ For enterprise implementations, which spanned disparate computer systems and numerous departments, complexity and integration proved to be overwhelming for most IT departments.

❑ Conflicting requirements, priorities, and the schedules of different departments and business units derailed many projects.

❑ Frequent cost overruns and delays.

All these problems became the drivers that led to the development and widespread growth of data marts in the past few years.

What is a data mart

A data mart is a small data warehouse, a decision support system, that aims to meet the needs of departments and smaller groups, rather than the complete enterprise. The design principles and objectives of a data mart and a data warehouse are the same. While both are decision support tools and have the same basic characteristics, such as being subject-oriented and integrated, a data mart is far smaller in size and scope. Typically, it is limited to one or two subjects (such as sales and finance), can be implemented within months, and cost less than $200,000.

A data mart has far less users and the size of its database, typically, is only a few gigabytes. This is relatively small compared to the typical data warehouses (storing hundreds of gigabytes) or the larger data warehouses (containing terabytes of data). A data mart requires simpler hardware and supporting technical infrastructure. Hence, it can be implemented by staff with less experience and technical skills.

Data mart characteristics

The following is a listing of important data mart characteristics and how they compare to those of a conventional data warehouse:

❑   A data mart aims to meet a department's needs while a data warehouse is designed for the enterprise. A data mart can be constructed by power users and other low-tech professionals.

❑   A data warehouse spans the entire organization, covers most subjects, is designed using an enterprise data model, and is constructed by a central professional team.

❑   A data mart is easy to design, build and test, which makes it cheaper to implement and maintain.

❑   A data mart, while it can store gigabytes of data, usually contains only a small part of an organization's data.

❑   A data warehouse needs to be planned and implemented as a huge project.

❑   An organization can build many data marts independently, in a staggered manner, as needs evolve. They need not be based on the enterprise data model structure. Data marts can be linked together, when required, but that task can be challenging.

❑ An organization can have many data marts—built by different teams without a common design. The result of independent construction is that integration, if required at a later stage, is difficult to achieve.

❑ While uniformity exists within a data warehouse project, it is missing when data marts sprout within a company because various implementation groups may use different processes, tools, hardware, and software.

❑ A data mart's source can be a data warehouse, another data mart, or an OLTP system.

Infrastructure: platforms and vendors

Data warehouses have been implemented on many platforms including Unix and Windows NT, which has been becoming popular in recent years. The implementation of a data warehouse project involves many technologies, tools, hardware, and software. They range from the very simple to the very sophisticated. While some vendors dominate in specific areas such as extraction or databases, and some have offerings across the range of products required to implement a data mart or data warehouse, no vendor dominates in all areas.

Some of the products that can be used to create and manage data marts include Oracle Data Mart Suite, IBM Enterprise Data Mart, Sybase Industry Warehouse Studio, SAP Business Warehouse, PeopleSoft Enterprise Warehouse, and SAS Warehouse Administrator.

Benefits of data marts

Data marts provide many benefits to organizations implementing them. They include:

❑ Easy and fast approval as departmental justification is easier to obtain

❑ Not dependent on IT budget

❑ Faster to build—months instead of years

❑ Cheaper and more affordable—can be built with departmental budgets (hundreds of thousands instead of millions required for an enterprise project)

❑ Low cost hardware and software can be used

❑ Simpler

❑ More focused

❑ Scalable

❑ Flexible

❑ Political conflict associated with **data warehouse** projects are avoided

❑ Fewer and less sophisticated resource **requirements**

❑ Ability to be linked to other data **marts, or data** warehouses, to form a distributed enterprise data warehouse

❑ Performance can be improved by storing **the data** closer to the users

Problems with data marts

While many benefits are associated with **implementing** data marts, they also have some problems associated with **them such as:**

❑ Development can be uncoordinated, **which creates** a hurdle when data marts are used as the building blocks for **creating an enter**prise data warehouse.

❑ Design is not as thorough as with a **data warehouse** due to superficial planning and inadequate, or no, **consideration for an** ultimate upgrade to an enterprise system.

❑ Cannot support a key requirement **of an enterprise** data warehouse—ability to analyze enterprise-wide data **across business** units. Consequently, the age-old problem with legacy systems **may also** afflict data marts—a question may yield different answers **depending on** which system was accessed, when it was accessed, and how the **query was** structured and executed.

❑ Design flaws and the number of **data extracts can** restrict scalability; may be unable to support massive data **volumes associated** with a data warehouse.

❑ Encourages clandestine development **and operations.**

❑ More work is required in reconciling **terms, definitions,** data, and business rules when data needs to be **migrated to an enter**prise data warehouse.

❑ Designed and built by less experienced **personnel,** which can affect the quality of the product.

❑ Can be expensive in the long-run.

❑ Growth of data marts creates more **redundant** and inconsistent data, which has a cost associated with it **and poses** problems when a data warehouse is to be upgraded.

❑ Multiple databases are required to **be maintained,** which requires greater breadth of technical skills.

❑ Extraction process can be different **for each data** mart.

❏ Activities such as extraction and processing are not centralized; activities can be duplicated and additional staff can be required for maintenance and support.

❏ Tools, software, hardware, and processes can be different for each data mart.

❏ Knowledge gained by one data mart group is not shared with the other groups.

DATA MART IMPLEMENTATION
Implementation approaches

There are three approaches that are commonly used to build data marts:

1. Top-down: Build an enterprise data warehouse (EDW) and then construct dependent data marts, which are its highly summarized subsets (Figure 2)

2. Bottom-up: Build independent data marts, whose foundation is the enterprise data model, which can then be used to construct an EDW (Figure 3)

3. Independent: Data marts are built randomly without any enterprise planning or consideration of a common data model; this approach can lead to anarchy over a period of time

Figure 2
Top-Down Architecture

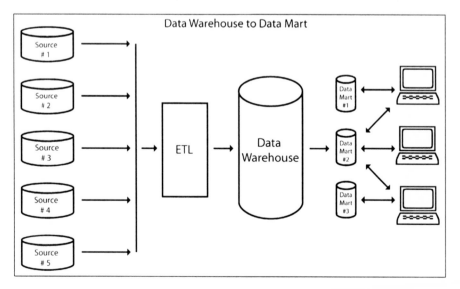

Figure 3
Bottom-Up Architecture

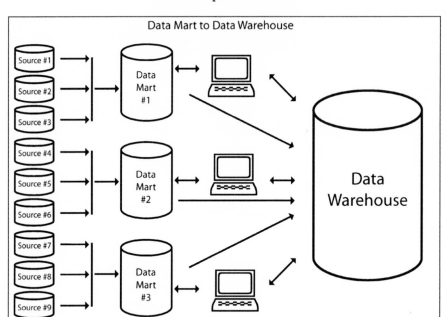

The characteristics defining the first approach, the top-down approach, are:

❑ It is methodology-based, which addresses important aspects such as modeling and implementation

❑ Provides an enterprise-wide view of the organization

❑ Avoids integration issues that characterize data warehouses derived from data marts

❑ Enterprise data warehouse drives the construction of dependent data marts, which permits better control and quality

❑ Inability to respond to business needs in time, long delivery cycle, high cost, project delays, cost overruns, and other issues associated with large projects

The characteristics defining the second approach, the bottom-up approach, are:

❑ Can meet some enterprise-wide needs as data marts can be combined seamlessly for viewing and analysis purposes

❏ Seamless and transparent integration, while possible, is technologically challenging; performance can be poor, especially if many data marts need to be integrated

❏ Can lead to the sprouting of data marts and data redundancy

❏ Lack of adherence to standards can cause major issues, especially integration problems, when an EDW is constructed from multiple data marts

❏ Fast implementation provides less time for analysis

Which approach to use

Both the top-down and bottom-up approaches have pros and cons. Each approach meets the needs of many types of users. The decision to select a particular approach is influenced by the relative importance of the various selection variables for the organization considering an implementation. For example, if the objective is to have something up and running quickly, or the budget is limited, the obvious choice is the data mart bottom-up approach. However, if strategic concerns and long-term considerations are driving the requirements, and the company is prepared to spend millions for a well designed system, the top-down approach for implementing an EDW might be the appropriate choice.

Extraction and loading

There are two primary ways in which data is usually loaded into a data mart:

1. Data is fed from an enterprise data warehouse to the data mart(s); any changes to the EDW is propagated to all associated data marts receiving its feeds

2. Data is fed by direct extract(s) from the operational systems(s)

There are two loading approaches: server-based and PC client-based. In the server-based approach, data extracted from the source system is loaded onto the data mart located on the server. However, the analysis software, used to access and analyze data on the server, is located on the user's PC.

In the client-based approach, both the data and the analysis software reside on the PC. Data is extracted from the source and loaded directly onto the PC. The problem with this approach is that since there can be hundreds of users, they may not update their PC resident databases simultaneously. Consequently, queries and reports can return different results and create a credibility issue.

Chapter 8

Multi-dimensionality

DRIVERS FOR MULTI-DIMENSIONAL ANALYSIS
Demand for improved data analysis

In the past two decades, organizations invested hundreds of billions of dollars for streamlining their business processes in order to gain a competitive edge. During that period, as the Internet exploded and many data-hungry applications such as ERP and CRM systems became widely deployed, huge amounts of data began to be collected. However, the captured data was barely analyzed and converted into information because the focus was on collecting data—not analyzing it.

The introduction of data warehousing technology shifted the focus from collecting data to analyzing the gold mine of data buried in corporate IT systems. However, the available analysis tools had some limitations. Consequently, many users felt an acute need for faster and more innovative techniques that would help them answer complex questions and support decision making. That need led to the development of the multi-dimensional analysis technique and associated tools.

Demand for multi-dimensional views and analysis
Limitations of traditional databases

Traditional relational databases, as well as spreadsheets, are based on a two-dimensional model of rows and columns. Such a model allows a user to view data in two dimensions, such as sales by region. However, data warehouse users rarely want to access data only through one dimension (or column). For example, it will be rare for a telecommunication company analyst to limit his analysis to determining the number of phone customers in a single state such as Pennsylvania. A typical analyst will perform far more comprehensive analysis such as comparing Pennsylvania phone customers through two dimensions—actual versus projected (number of customers).

This scenario can become complicated as more dimensions are added. For example, the analyst might like to determine the number of customers who subscribed to both home and wireless service in the past year. Additionally, he might like to compare the answer generated by his query to the historical results in order to determine a trend or aberration. To generate his query using traditional databases, the analyst would have to access data in different tables and then perform complex table joins—a task that would be beyond the capabilities of ordinary users.

Need to analyze through multi-dimensions

Most data warehouse queries are multi-dimensional, which use multiple criteria against multiple columns, because the two-dimensional view of data limits the type of analysis that can be performed. Two-dimensional views cannot support the requirement to understand the relationship between multi-dimensions such as sales, geography (region), and distribution channel. In a relational database, analyzing multiple dimensions would require the setup of a series of tables (sales, regions, and distribution channels). These tables would first be joined and then accessed through complex SQL code in order to analyze the cost trends over time.

The need for joins, which are not difficult for programmers to implement, forces users to consider the data structure. Multi-dimensional analysis overcomes this limitation by accessing data through more than one dimension or column (criteria). For example, it can enable analysis of sales by product by region over time. It can even permit analysis of additional dimensions such as sales by product by region over time by color.

UNDERSTANDING MULTI-DIMENSIONALITY

The dimensional model overcomes the limitations of relational databases, which are organized in a two-dimensional format. The dimensional model is based on a structure organized by dimensions, such as sales or geography, and is represented by a multi-dimensional array or cube. This model, which over-comes the two dimension limitation of relational databases, provides an intu-itive way of organizing and selecting data for querying and analysis. A multi-dimensional model:

❑ Is representative of the company's business model

❑ Provides a view that is business rather than technical; users can concen-trate on the business instead of the tool

❑ Enables slicing and dicing, which provides the ability to analyze data using different scenarios such as sales by products, region, channel, and period

❑ Permits data to be easily analyzed across any dimension and any level of aggregation

❑ Is flexible and permits powerful analytical processing

Dimensions

A dimension represents an attribute such as product, region, or time. All data warehouses have one common dimension—time. A spreadsheet is the simplest example of a two-dimensional model. The spreadsheet row and column names are the "dimensions" while the numeric data in it are the "facts." A time dimen-sion can include all months, quarters, years, etc., while a geography dimension can include all countries, regions, and cities. A dimension acts like an index for identifying values in a multi-dimensional array. If the number of dimensions used is increased, greater is the level of detail that can be queried.

If a single member is selected from all dimensions, then a single cell is defined. A three-dimensional model is represented as a cubic structure in which each dimension forms a side of the cube. In a dimensional model, data is organized according to a business user's perspective with common dimensions being time, region, products, distribution or sales channels, and budget.

Figure 4 represents a three-dimensional model with region, product, and time dimensions. Figures 5 and 6 represent multiple dimension views—by brand and region. Figures 7 and 8 show the same data sliced in different ways—along a single cube as well as along three dimensions (region, product, time).

Figure 4
3-Dimensional Model

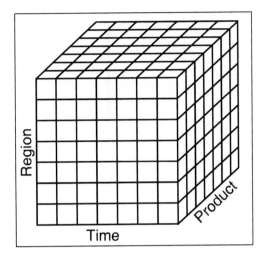

Figure 5
Multiple-Dimension Views—Brand

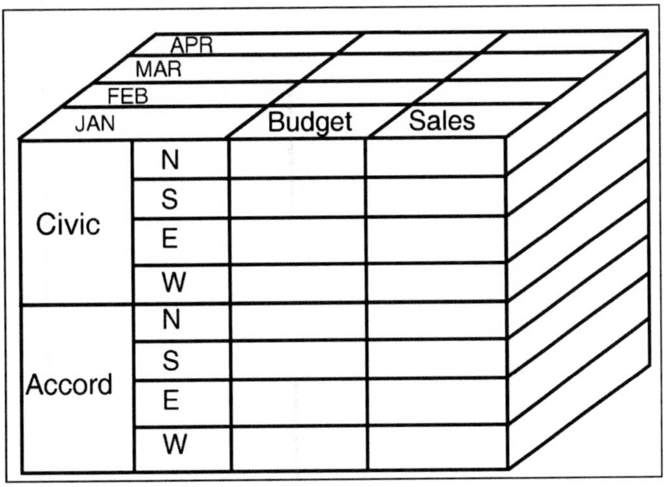

Figure 6
Multiple-Dimension Views—Region

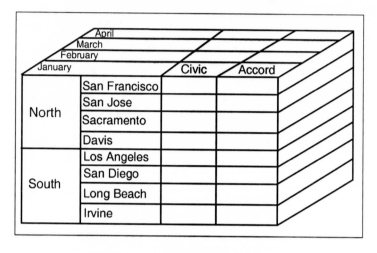

Figure 7
Slicing and Dicing (Single Cell)

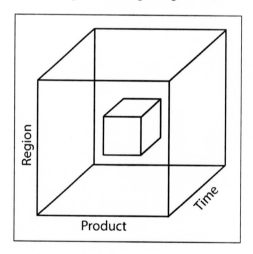

Figure 8
Slicing and Dicing Along Multiple Dimensions

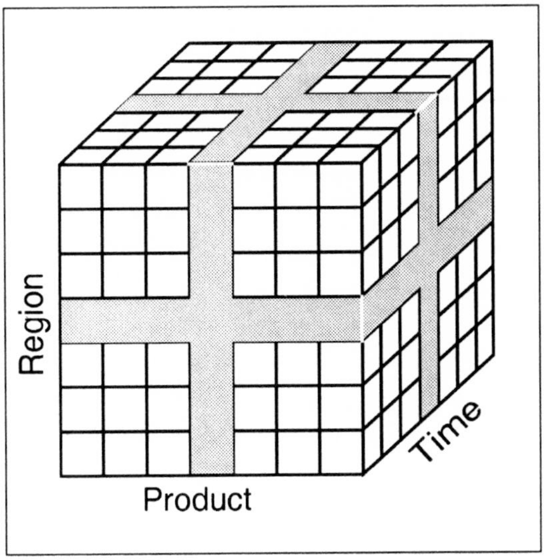

Facts

The values in the array in a dimensional model, which change over time, are called facts. Examples of facts, which are used to measure performance, include sales, units sold, costs, and shipments. Fact tables, which are the focus of dimensional queries, contain two types of fields:

❑ Fields that store the foreign key which connects each fact to the appropriate value in each dimension

❑ Fields that store individual facts such as price, quantity, salary, etc.

Characteristics of fact and dimension tables

The following are the defining characteristic of facts and dimensions:

❑ Fact table characteristics:
  o Fact table consists of multiple columns and a large number of rows (can be millions)
  o Is the primary table which contains the numeric data—measurements such as price, cost, profit, and salary

- o Holds the "real" quantitative data—the data being queried; typically holds atomic and aggregate data such as the number of cars sold
- o Fact table contains all of the attributes to be measured
- o Fact table row corresponds to a measurement
- o Measurement takes place at the intersection of all the dimensions such as month, product, and region
- o Fact represents a business measure; fact attributes contain measurable numeric values (which are normally additive)
- o Numerical measures are restricted to fact tables
- o Facts can be operated upon (summed, averaged, aggregated, etc.)

❏ Dimension table characteristics:
- o Reflects business dimensions such as product, region, and distribution channel
- o Contains a primary key that connects it to the fact table
- o Dimensional attributes provide links between the fact table and its associated dimension tables
- o Contains descriptive data reflecting business dimensions; dimensional attributes provide description of each row in the fact table
- o Groups descriptive attributes about the facts; dimension table has many attribute fields; each field describes individual characteristics of the dimension; for example, attributes of product dimension could be description, size, color, weight, type, etc.
- o Are used to guide the selection of rows from the fact table
- o Dimensions permit categorization of transactions; example, customer dimension can be used to analyze procurement by location, frequency, etc.
- o ables are smaller as they have fewer number of rows
- o Tables are de-normalized but that does not increase storage significantly as the dimension tables are very small compared to the fact table

Multi-dimensional analysis

Multi-dimensional analysis is a powerful analytical tool that can provide insight not possible through two-dimensional analysis. The following example shows how multi-dimensional analysis can be used to analyze the sales for a car dealership using multiple dimensions.

The car dealership is split into two sales regions: North and South. The consolidated total sales for each region are shown in Table 1:

Table 1: Single dimension	
Region	Sales (millions)
North	237
South	226

In Table 1, there is only one fact (sales) which is related to a single dimension (region). The only dimension in this case (region) is used for aggregating its associated fact (sales). If the car dealer desires to perform detailed analysis, he can drill-down so that the sales dollars for each region for each quarter, as shown in Table 2, can be viewed.

Table 2: Two dimensions		
Region	Time (quarter)	Sales (millions)
North	Q1	56
	Q2	61
	Q3	60
	Q4	60
South	Q1	52
	Q2	57
	Q3	62
	Q4	55

Table 2 relates one fact (sales) to two dimensions—region and time (quarter). It shows the aggregated sales dollars associated with each of the eight combinations of region and time dimensions.

If the car dealer wants to analyze his sales even more comprehensively, he can use a third dimension (model) as shown in Table 3—which relates one fact (sales) to three dimensions (region, time, and model). Table 3 shows the aggregated sales (facts) for each combination of region, time, and model.

Table 3: Three dimensions			
Region	Time (quarter)	Model	Sales (millions)
North	Q1	Accord	23
	Q1	Civic	33
	Q2	Accord	27
	Q2	Civic	34
	Q3	Accord	29
	Q3	Civic	31
	Q4	Accord	24
	Q4	Civic	36
South	Q1	Accord	21
	Q1	Civic	31
	Q2	Accord	23
	Q2	Civic	34
	Q3	Accord	27
	Q3	Civic	35
	Q4	Accord	22
	Q4	Civic	33

Multi-dimensional database

A multi-dimensional database is a type of proprietary database that stores data in an array format, rather than tables. The data is organized and stored by pre-defined dimensions, which permit users to view it in multiple dimensions that correspond to easy-to-understand business dimensions. The enabling of a business view of the data permits users to navigate through various dimensions and data levels, which can uncover important trends.

Multi-dimensional databases are designed to support multi-dimensional queries run for analyzing complex questions. However, while a multi-dimensional database supports slice and dice capabilities, its proprietary solution is a drawback that can prevent or limit the use of available query tools.

DATA WAREHOUSE DATABASE DESIGNS
Star schema

The star schema design, which is commonly used for designing data warehouse databases, supports analytical processing. It takes its name from the star-like arrangement of entities. The star schema is the design most frequently used to implement a multi-dimensional model in a relational database. Its structure consists of a central fact table with keys to many dimension tables (Figure 9). The following characteristics are associated with a star schema:

❑ It contains two types of tables: Fact (or major) and Dimension (or minor)

❑ One dimension represents one table

❑ Dimension tables surround the fact table

❑ Dimension tables are de-normalized

❑ Dimension tables are linked to the fact table through unique keys (one per dimension table)

❑ Every dimension key uniquely identifies a row in the dimension table associated with it

❑ A fact table's specific row is uniquely identified by the dimension keys

❑ Uses many ERD components such as entities, attributes, cardinality, primary keys, and relationships connectors

The star schema design has many advantages. It favors de-normalization for optimizing speed. Due to de-normalization of the time dimension, a significant reduction occurs in the number of tables that need to be joined when time-based queries are executed. A star schema's performance is good because one large table needs to be joined with a few small tables, resulting in a fast response time. The star schema reflects how business users view data, makes metadata navigation easier for both programmers and end-users, and permits more versatility in the selection of front-end tools.

Snowflake schema

If a dimension table has subcategories or more than one level of dimension tables, and more efficient access is required, a snowflake schema can be used. The snowflake schema, which is derived from the star schema, adds a hierarchical structure to the dimension tables (Figure 10). It is more normalized and complex.

Figure 9
Star Schema

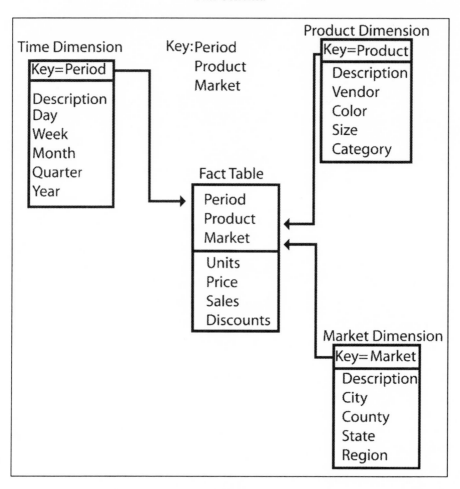

Figure 10
Snowflake Schema

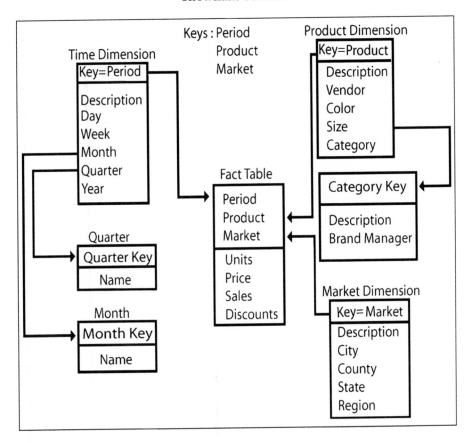

Chapter 9

OLAP

ONLINE ANALYTICAL PROCESSING
What is OLAP

Online analytical processing, OLAP, is an analytical technique that combines data access tools with an analytical database engine. In contrast to the simple rows and columns structure of relational databases, upon which most data warehouses are built, OLAP uses a multi-dimensional view of data such as sales by brand, season, and store. OLAP, which works on data aggregations, uses calculations and transformations to perform its analytical tasks. There are two types of OLAP system architectures:

❑ Multi-dimensional OLAP (MOLAP):
   o uses a multi-dimensional database in which data is stored multi-dimensionally
   o products include Essbase (Hyperion), Powerplay (Cognos), and Commander (Comshare)
❑ Relational OLAP (ROLAP):
   o uses a relational database that is accessed directly
   o MicroStrategy's DSS Server is a ROLAP product

OLAP database server

An OLAP server stores data as well as the relationships between the data. It is optimized for ad hoc query processing and data manipulation. An OLAP server is designed to work with multi-dimensional data structures, which can be visualized as cubes of data (and cubes within cubes), with the following characteristics:

- ❏ A cell is a single point in a cube
- ❏ Each data item is located, and accessed, based on the intersection of the dimensions defining it
- ❏ Each side of a cube is a dimension that represents an attribute or category such as product, region, channel, or time period
- ❏ Each cell contains aggregated data that relates the elements along each dimension
- ❏ Using the dimension numbers that define them, data items can be easily located and accessed
- ❏ An intermediate server can be used to store pre-calculations

An OLAP server's key characteristic is its calculation engine. An OLAP server can extract data in real-time from relational or other databases and, when required, manipulate it. However, the more common and preferred method is to physically store the data on the OLAP server in multi-dimensional format. A database which stores data in multi-dimensional format is known as a multi-dimensional database (MDDB).

BENEFITS AND FEATURES
OLAP benefits

OLAP technology enables decision makers to access data quickly, efficiently, interactively, and in innovative ways without first having to understand the data structure or technical details. The data, which is presented in dimensions as business users view it, can be queried and analyzed using different views. Compared to data warehouses based on relational database technology, OLAP systems have an additional feature—the ability to perform "what if" analysis, a powerful tool that can simulate the effect of decisions. For example, OLAP can answer a question like, "what will be the impact on airline ticket sales if the price of jet fuel rises by $0.15 per gallon, one hub is closed, and another fuel distribution center is added to the system."

The following are some of the benefits that OLAP technology can provide:

- ❏ Enable users to identify key trends and factors driving their businesses—such as helping them understand changes in buying patterns and customer preferences

- ❏ Ability to perform complex calculations and trend analysis
- ❏ Ability to manipulate data with many inter-relationships
- ❏ Insulate users from SQL language and the relational model
- ❏ Improve query performance; massive amounts of data can be analyzed rapidly
- ❏ Improve scalability
- ❏ Support a wide range of tools
- ❏ Automate maintenance of indexes and summaries
- ❏ Decrease demand for reports from IT
- ❏ Fast deployment
- ❏ Application in a wide range of applications such as forecasting, profitability analysis, customer analysis, budgeting, and marketing analysis
- ❏ Increase productivity of individuals and organizations

Desired OLAP features

There are many characteristics and features desired in an OLAP system including:

- ❏ User perspective: data should be transparent to the users
- ❏ Ease of use
- ❏ Intuitive data manipulation
- ❏ Easy and fast deployment
- ❏ Seamless presentation of historical, projected, and derived data
- ❏ Reasonable cost
- ❏ Cost-effective maintenance
- ❏ Ability to perform operations against single or multiple dimensions (aggregate, summarize, and derive data)
- ❏ Powerful calculation capabilities
- ❏ Support for statistical and analytical functions
- ❏ Support more than simple aggregation or roll-ups such as share calculations (% of total) and allocations
- ❏ Support for large data sets and unlimited dimensions and aggregation levels
- ❏ Time intelligence which supports analysis such as year-to-date and period-over-period
- ❏ Provide secure and concurrent access to data

❑ Consistent and fast query performance

❑ Flexible reporting; consistent reporting performance

❑ Integration with desktop tools

❑ Scalability—large data volumes as well as the number of concurrent users

❑ Permit data to be read while updates are occurring

WHERE OLAP FITS IN
OLAP versus data warehouse

A typical data warehouse basically stores data in a de-normalized relational format. However, OLAP has a multi-dimensional structure which can be leveraged to transform data into meaningful and strategic information. A data warehouse can be classified as informational compared to OLAP, which is analytical. While various tools can be used to access a data warehouse and run queries against it, OLAP is relatively versatile and goes far beyond data access. Its vast range of capabilities include drill-down, slice and dice, as well as complex calculations and modeling. However, in comparison to a data warehouse database, which can be terabytes in size, an OLAP server will typically be far smaller—in the gigabytes range.

OLAP versus OLTP

Online transaction processing systems are primarily used to run the business operations of a company. OLTP functions are performed by production applications that routinely capture business transactions in diverse areas such as inventory management, order processing, human resources, production planning, budgeting, etc. On the other hand, OLAP systems work with data that is geared towards decision making, especially long-term strategic decisions. Examples of OLAP applications include trend analysis, sales forecasting, and customer profiling.

Table 4	
OLTP	OLAP
Contains a snapshot of the current data (6-24 months)	Requires a history of transactions spread over many years (5-20 years)
Updated continuously	Static data
Can have errors or missing data	Validated and complete data
Processes millions of transactions daily	Updated periodically through batch processing—usually once per day
Uses Entity-Relationship Diagram	Uses multi-dimensional model

MOLAP versus ROLAP

In multi-dimensional OLAP (MOLAP), data is stored in a special OLAP database server, after being extracted from various sources, in pre-aggregated cubic format. This data remains static until an extract from the source system(s) adds more data to it. In contrast to this approach, relational OLAP (ROLAP), does not use an intermediate server because it can work directly against the relational database. Consequently, it can perform analysis on the fly.

MOLAP performs well with 10 or fewer dimensions while ROLAP can scale considerably higher. ROLAP is not restricted by the number of dimensions, type or number of users, database size, or complexity of analysis. It can perform ad hoc queries and aggregate data much faster—even with constantly changing and a much larger amount of data. Another ROLAP advantage is that it can leverage parallel scalable relational databases. The disadvantages of ROLAP are that it has limited scalability, places a heavy load on the server, and is expensive to maintain.

MOLAP, which starts seeing performance degradation at about 50GB of data or 10 dimensions, is more suitable for financial applications where the data can be broken down and is smaller. ROLAP is more suitable for applications where a huge amount of data needs to be analyzed, such as marketing and point-of-sale. ROLAP products are provided by a number of vendors including MicroStrategy, Data Dynamics, IBM, and Information Advantage (Sterling Software). MOLAP vendors include Comshare, Hyperion, and IBM.

OTHER TYPES OF OLAP
Database OLAP (DOLAP)

Database online analytical processing, DOLAP, is another type of OLAP. Its defining characteristic is that an OLAP engine resides in the database, which provides the fastest querying. An advantage of this technique is flexibility as users do not have to precisely define their requirements in advance—as required by MOLAP. Another DOLAP advantage is that it can store more data than MOLAP while the disadvantage is that it is slower. Products in this category are provided by a number of vendors including Business Objects, Brio Technology, and Cognos.

Hybrid OLAP (HOLAP)

Hybrid OLAP (HOLAP) combines the features of ROLAP and MOLAP. It takes advantage of the superior processing of MOLAP with the ability of ROLAP to work with greater data volumes. HOLAP stores data in both a relational database and multi-dimensional database (MDDB). Either database can be used depending on the type of processing required—data processing or ad hoc querying. In HOLAP, the aggregations are stored using a MOLAP strategy while the source data, which is far greater in volume, is stored using a ROLAP strategy. The result is that the least storage is used while enabling very fast processing.

The hybrid OLAP system combines the performance and functionality of the MDDB with the ability to access detail data, which provides greater value to some categories of users. However, HOLAP implementations are typically supported by a single vendor's databases and, also, are fairly complex to deploy and maintain. Additionally, they can be somewhat restrictive in terms of their mobility. Products in this category are provided by a number of vendors including Microsoft, Crystal Decisions, Oracle, and Pilot Software.

MULTI-DIMENSIONAL TOOLS
Types of OLAP tools

The three most common types of multi-dimensional OLAP tools are:

❑ Spreadsheets which present data in a cross-tab view that is familiar to business users; the amount of data that can be accessed through such a tool is limited

❑ Client-based multi-dimensional databases (such as Pablo), which retain pre-calculated consolidated data in PC memory; the magnitude of data that can be accessed through such tools ranges in the megabytes

❑ Server-based multi-dimensional databases (such as Essbase, Express, and Holos), which can handle gigabytes of data and implement various performance and storage optimization techniques

All the tools have certain limitations in terms of functionality, compatibility, scalability, performance, and cost. For example, while ROLAP systems store data in standard relational databases, their schema can be quite complex. A proprietary data structure, despite being stored in a relational database, can make a product incompatible with another product's schema. Additionally, ROLAPs make a tradeoff in terms of significantly reduced performance and functionality, as well as the cost of implementation, while outperforming in the ability to handle larger amounts of data compared to MOLAPs. Therefore, tool selection should be based on an evaluation of the specific application being considered.

Selecting a vendor

Selecting a vendor involves many variables, which should be carefully evaluated before the selection is made. These include:

❑ Size: established vendors provide confidence that they will still be around after a few years

❑ Commitment: the amount of revenues that the OLAP business generates for the vendor and the importance attached to it

❑ Preference: one-stop shopping or best-of-breed

In recent years, the tools business has grown very competitive. At this time, there are many OLAP vendors including Oracle, IBM, Microsoft, Business Objects, SAS, and MicroStrategy (ROLAP).

Chapter 10

Planning a Data Warehouse Project

PLANNING AND APPROACH
Understand why the project is being undertaken

Before embarking on a data warehouse project, determine why the project is being undertaken as well as management expectations. Is the need departmental or enterprise? Are operational, strategic or tactical needs to be fulfilled by the data warehouse? Answers to these questions will clarify the project objectives and can influence important decisions regarding scope, architecture, methodology, tools, etc.

Justification

Data warehouse projects used to be initiated with R&D budgets, when the technology was immature and unproven, without formal cost justification. However, it is now a mature technology and, therefore, should be approached with the same thoroughness and preparation associated with any application development project. A data warehouse project should not be undertaken unless it has been justified by a cost/benefit analysis. The analysis should be performed by a consultant or someone who is respected within the organization. A well-justified project improves the probability of success and buy-in, especially if the justification is well communicated.

Project prerequisites

A data warehouse project should not be implemented unless:

❑ Demand, strategic and operational, has been determined

❑ Criteria for valuing the data warehouse has been determined

❑ Cost is justified

❑ Source(s) and availability of required legacy and external data have been studied

❑ Data warehouse size and type have been determined

❑ Existing and required infrastructure have been evaluated

❑ Location has been determined

❑ Operational challenges have been identified

❑ Decision to build or buy the data warehouse has been taken

Evaluate potential impact

The implementation of a data warehouse introduces new technologies and retires older ones. The new architecture, which typically is a radical departure from the existing infrastructure, is the foundation upon which the new information architecture is based. It can impact company employees at all levels, ranging from senior executives to end-users, as well as IT staff. Therefore, it is imperative that the potential impact of the implementation on the organization should be evaluated.

Obtain sponsorship

A typical data warehouse project is very large, has unique characteristics, and is very risky if it is not properly managed or lacks sponsorship. A data warehouse project must have a sponsor who should be drawn from the functional side—not the IT department. The sponsor should have a vested interest in the project. He should be respected and be capable of acting decisively, providing resources when required, forcing compromises, and enforcing decisions. He should communicate his commitment to the project and keep a close eye on its progress and, when required, step in without any delay.

Evaluate readiness for implementation

Data warehouse projects are not easy to plan and implement. An organization considering a data warehouse implementation must be prepared to adopt radical changes which can affect the architecture, techniques, tools, as well as operation and maintenance. Therefore, before deciding to proceed with such a project, management's commitment and the organization's readiness for change must be determined. If management lacks commitment, the project should be delayed until the conditions are more favorable.

Consider using a data mart approach

Evaluate the two alternative implementation approaches: building a large data warehouse in classical fashion or starting off with a data mart. In the big bang approach, the requirements and scope are massive, and the data warehouse covers many subjects—which can be implemented either simultaneously or in phases after the overall design has been completed. In the data mart approach, which has modest departmental focus, the design effort is limited and only one or two subjects are selected for initial implementation. Both methods have pros and cons, which should be thoroughly evaluated to determine the best approach for implementing the data warehouse solution.

IDENTIFYING BARRIERS, CHALLENGES, AND RISKS

Data warehouse projects are more complex and difficult to implement than conventional application development projects. Before a project is started, the challenges and risks associated with deploying a data warehouse should be identified. Failure to understand the unique nature of a data warehouse project, and its impact on the organization, significantly increases risk and the probability of failure. The challenges and risks that typically derail a data warehouse project are discussed in the following sections.

Barriers

An important planning task is the identification of the barriers to implementation. Typically, the barriers are of two types. The first type is political and cultural, which can be attributed to senior executives, functional department managers, data owners, IT, and business users. The second type of barrier is technical, which is comparatively easy to identify, evaluate, and manage. If these barriers to implementation are identified in time, the risk to the project is reduced.

Complexity

A data warehouse project is considerably more complex and difficult to execute than a conventional application development project. It is technologically complex due to the greater number, and sophistication, of tools required to implement the system as well as integration challenges. Such a project requires many high-level skilled technical resources. It also involves many departments and groups, whose needs and requirements can be in conflict due to different priorities and politics. Consequently, such factors can combine to create a complex project that is under tremendous pressure to be delivered on time and within budget.

Integration

A data warehouse is fed data from multiple sources which can be residing on different platforms and systems. The data from the various sources is ultimately integrated inside the data warehouse after undergoing some operations. The overall data warehouse process uses a variety of technologies including databases, ETL tools, middleware, front-end reporting tools, networks, etc. Integrating all of them is a complex task and a challenge—from a technical as well as business perspective.

Financial risk

A data warehouse project is always exposed to two risks: cost overrun and schedule slippage—both of which increase financial risk. They have a negative impact on resources, force scope reduction, lead to competing demand for funds from other successful projects, cause a window of opportunity to be missed, etc. In the worst scenario, a delayed or over budget project can be scrapped.

Resource and schedule constraints

The resources for a data warehouse project are made available for a specific period, after negotiations, by various departments and organizations. Any delay in using the resources can, in many cases, effectively mean that they will not be available when required. The complex and time-intensive nature of a data warehouse project, with hundreds of interdependent tasks, requires that schedule constraints must be carefully monitored for ensuring project success.

Politics

As a data warehouse project involves many departments including business entities and IT, with conflicting priorities and agendas, it can face serious political issues and associated risks. Major politics can impact such a project at every step including selecting/prioritizing the subjects for implementation, requirements determination, project team selection, access tool selection, etc. Therefore, the project should be led by someone who has superior project management skills and is politically savvy.

Design differences

The design of a data warehouse database is fundamentally different compared to that of an OLTP system database. The primary design objective of a data warehouse, with its decision support and analysis requirements, is querying and reporting. A data warehouse is required to respond to complex and ad hoc queries, rather than provide simple reporting.

A data warehouse aims to extract information from a database rather than capture data. Hence, it places emphasis on analytical tasks such as drill-down capabilities, slice and dice, etc. On the other hand, an OLTP system's primary objective is to capture and store transaction data, which leads to its performance requirement that the database be updated efficiently. An OLTP system database stores only current operational data, which typically ranges from six months to two years. A data warehouse contains current as well as historical data which increases its size tremendously and, consequently, impacts its performance. It also contains a time element, which makes it more complex.

Complexity and size of data warehouses

Data warehouse databases contain a large number of tables which are characterized by complex relationships. When a query is executed, the tables required to process it are joined selectively to produce the desired result. To use the data warehouse, non-technical business users do not need to understand the database structure, names of the tables or their relationships, or how to create an SQL query. However, the data warehouse architect has to design a schema that can be presented to the users in an easy-to-understand, non-technical, format that uses business terms. This is a complex undertaking that requires both technical and business knowledge.

Data warehouse databases are very large. In some cases, they are huge, in the terabyte range, because they have to store data for very lengthy periods. The data stored in data warehouses is fed from many sources, internal and external, which makes the database structurally complex. Also very complicated is the process to extract, transform, and load data into the data warehouse.

Difficulty in managing projects

A data warehouse project cannot be handled like a typical conventional application development project that is managed and implemented by IT. Due to its nature, a data warehouse project is business-driven—not led by IT. The number and types of users involved with such a project can be quite varied. Stakeholders can be across divisions, geographies, business units, and departments. Personnel involved with the project can include consultants, business analysts, IT technical staff, line managers, senior management, end-users, and ordinary workers. Usually, many project staff members lack data warehouse project experience, which creates a challenging management environment.

Business and technical skills requirement

Many types of skills, technical and business, are required to plan and implement a data warehouse project. The technical skills span legacy systems, data conversion and migration, operating systems, databases, networking, front-end access tools, client/server and web technologies, etc. Knowledge of the business and decision support systems is also a requirement. Other skills required include organization, the ability to work in a team environment, multi-tasking, work with deadlines and under pressure, and good communications.

Decision making capabilities

During the life of a data warehouse project, many critical decisions need to be made. Therefore, an assessment of the decision making capabilities of the project staff must be made. If the staff is unable to make decisions, due to lack of delegation of responsibilities or inability to make decisions (due to the corporate culture or personality), it will be difficult to complete the project on time. The project team members must be able to act quickly and decisively.

GETTING READY FOR THE PROJECT
Determine project principles

The guiding principles, which are a set of goals, must be defined at this stage. They can be referred to and used throughout the project, especially when conflicts arise over misinterpreted objectives. The project business drivers also need to be defined at an early stage. They provide the means for quantitatively measuring success against metrics. Examples include revenue growth, customer retention rate, improvement in efficiency, decrease in product failure rate or returns, etc.

Perform skills assessment

The start of a data warehouse project should be preceded by skills assessment. The skills levels and capabilities, of the potential project team members and ultimate end-users, need to be determined. Both technical and business skills assessment must be performed. The skills assessment exercise helps pinpoint deficiencies and indicates the areas where external resources may be required for implementation and/or providing support after the data warehouse becomes operational.

Select implementation partner

There are three common approaches to implementing a data warehouse:
- Using in-house staff
- Using a vendor
- Teaming with a partner

Unless the company staff has data warehouse or data mart implementation experience, the first option can mean a longer implementation time and considerably higher risk (cost and time). The lack of technical know-how can lead to a flawed design, poor performance, extraction and loading problems, other technical issues, selection of wrong tools, etc.

With an experienced vendor, the implementation can be faster and smoother. However, maintaining the system can be an issue after the vendor leaves due to inadequate knowledge transfer to the operational staff. Therefore, upgrading such a system will be more expensive compared to a system implemented by in-house staff.. Also, there will be a greater need for ongoing and future consulting/training costs.

Typically, the third approach is the best because the system is implemented by a skilled consulting partner in close collaboration with in-house staff, who pick up both business and technical skills. The key to a successful implementation is to select a partner who, besides designing and implementing the data warehouse, can also provide on-going support.

Select project leader

An implementation leader should be selected who possesses the qualities associated with a successful project manager. The person selected for such a position should have a reputation for completing projects on time and within budget. The project manager should be a decisive leader and must be given adequate authority so that the project does not suffer due to the lack of adequate decision making authority.

Determine project team requirements and roles

The implementation of a data warehouse project requires many skills—technical and business. The typical positions that are associated with such a project include:

❑ Sponsor: Senior executive responsible for the overall project who, typically, is the chairman of the Steering Committee

❑ Steering Committee: Responsible for ensuring that the project runs smoothly and is in sync with the corporate business and IT strategy; consists of functional staff drawn from various business areas as well as IT representative

❑ Project Manager: Responsible for project's strategic direction and ensuring that budget and schedule are adhered to; manages the project and project team; provides progress reports

❑ Functional sponsor: Executive responsible for the business within the specific functional area

❑ Functional representatives: Functional business users and end-users associated with the project in various capacities; may be working full-time or part-time during various project phases—from planning through user acceptance

❑ Project team: Implements the project and executes specific project plan tasks; includes business team members (subject matter experts, business analysts, functional staff, etc.) as well as technical team members (architect, developers, data warehouse administrator, etc.)

❑ IT support staff (during implementation): Responsible for the IT infrastructure and software requirements

❑ IT support staff (after go-live): Responsible for maintaining the system and infrastructure

Select project team members

The project team members required to fill the identified roles within the project are selected keeping in mind the following:

❑ Team members should have suitable characteristics that can enable them to meet the requirements of a challenging project; they must understand the company's business, needs, and requirements

❑ Should be capable decision makers

❑ Must be able to allocate time to the project; team members should not have dual requirements that interfere with their project tasks

❑ Preferably have a stake in the implementation

Chapter 11

Building and Operating a Data Warehouse

PROJECT IMPLEMENTATION

The implementation of a data warehouse is executed in a series of steps, that need to be clearly identified in a project plan, which are described in the following sections. If the work plan is not diligently adhered to, the project will be jeopardized and the potential to incur delays and cost overruns will increase significantly.

In the past decade, as data warehouse technology has matured, the approach to implement it has also changed. Instead of an iterative methodology, structured methodologies are being used to implement data warehouse projects. The various methodologies reflect the experiences that implementers have gained over the years. The important point to note is that an implementation must not be carried out without a formal methodology—the roadmap for ensuring that the project is executed according to sound project principles.

Planning

An unplanned project is a blueprint for disaster. Before a data warehouse implementation starts, it should be preceded by detailed planning as described in the previous chapter. The planning phase must define the scope, specifications, as well as specific responsibilities for the client, vendor, and consulting partner(s). Scope creep is a major issue with data warehouse projects. Since the scope can easily get out of hand, either before or after it has been finalized, it must be controlled. Data warehouse project scope can be managed by limiting the number of subjects to be implemented, number of departments to be included, number of data sources, data source quality, data warehouse size, number or types of users, analysis techniques, and platform to be implemented (existing or new).

The project plan is created in the planning phase. It contains the project schedule and identifies the activities to be performed for implementing the data warehouse. The project deliverables are identified in this phase and the resource requirements, internal as well as consulting, are also defined.

In many projects, a number of tasks listed in the analysis and design phase sections are initially performed at a preliminary or high level in the planning phase. Subsequently, they are addressed more thoroughly in the analysis or design phase. These include tasks such as database selection (relational/multidimensional), capacity planning, data refresh and update strategy, archiving strategy, etc.—which can impact implementation as well as routine operations and maintenance.

In some projects, the implementation strategy, top-down or bottom-up, is also determined in the planning phase. However, the selected or preferred strategy can be changed based on the results of the analysis phase.

Analysis

In the analysis phase, a very comprehensive study of the business is conducted. To understand the business, a wide range of personnel are interviewed. They include executives, managers, business analysts, and functional experts from various business units being considered for the data warehouse implementation.

In this phase, the information needs of the business users, the requirements, are analyzed. This involves analyzing the current situation to determine "what" the system does. The next step is to turn the high-level business requirements into specific requirements of what the system must do and what its characteristics should be.

The analysis phase leads to the definition of the architecture (2-tier, 3-tier, or web) as well as the processes for linking the data sources, the data warehouse, and the front-end data access tools. The analysis phase can lead to scope modification (increase/decrease). It can also impact the pre-determined, or yet-to-be selected, implementation strategy (top-down or bottom-up).

Some of the other important items that are typically determined or defined in the analysis phase include the:

❑ Subject areas (customers, orders, sales, bookings, etc.)

❑ Desired features and functions

❑ Logical data model

❑ Dimensional business model (facts, dimensions, hierarchies, and relationships)

❑ Dimensions of potential interest

❑ Operational/Other data required to be moved into the data warehouse (customers, bookings, sales, external data, etc.)

❑ Data sources and elements (legacy and other sources—external or internal)

❑ Data requirements (which data is to be used)

❑ Data levels (detailed versus summarized, granularity)

❑ Historical data requirements

❑ Data flows: how the sources (operational systems/other data marts/EDW) feed the data warehouse

❑ Sizing (to determine data warehouse capacity)

❑ Range of queries expected

❑ Query and reporting requirements

❑ Existing and planned platforms and processes

❑ Impact on existing infrastructure (hardware, software, networks, etc.) and personnel

Design

In the design phase, a determination is made of "how" the system will be implemented. The primary design consideration is to develop an optimal solution within the various constraints such as cost, schedule, and infrastructure. The impact of every major design issue, on the implementation as well as future operation and maintenance, is studied.

Some of the common design issues addressed in this phase include the following:

❑ How much data is to be extracted and transformed

❑ Should complete files, or only changes, be imported

❑ Should update frequency be event or time driven

❑ Aggregation

❑ Backup and recovery procedures

❑ Data distribution and replication (to ensure that when data is changed, all copies of the database reflect the changes and remain in sync)

In this phase, the physical data model for the data warehouse is developed. The high-level data model identifies the major subject areas as well as the relationships between the major subjects. The mid-level data model identifies attributes, groupings of attributes, as well as the relationships of groupings of attributes. The low-level data model, which is ready for physical database implementation, includes the physical characteristics of attributes.

The physical database design involves designing the database, fact and relationship tables, data de-normalization, indexing, etc. The data source physical data models are mapped to the physical model of the data warehouse (source to target). The data mapping, transformation, and integration tasks involve:

❑ Defining the sources

❑ Determining the logic and rules

❑ Determining the file layouts

❑ Data formatting and translation; creating the transformation specifications

❑ Mapping the source(s) to the target

Implementation

In this phase, the construction of the physical data warehouse, as per specifications and project scope, is carried out. Before the construction step is carried out, various components of the proposed data warehouse system need to be evaluated and selected based upon a timeline specified in the project plan. Some components may already be installed within the existing IT infrastructure while others, including hardware and software, may need to be procured.

The physical data warehouse, the database that will hold all the imported source data, is created from the logical and physical database designs in a number of steps. The important steps include data extraction, transformation, staging, loading, validation, and testing. An important task that precedes ETL is the development of programs that perform a variety of tasks, which can also be performed by a variety of off-the-shelf tools, such as:

❑ Normalizing and building tables

❑ Modifying/Refreshing the warehouse

❑ Extracting, transforming, and loading data

❑ Summarizing and aggregating data

Other important tasks accomplished in the implementation phase include:

❑ Installing/upgrading the physical infrastructure (network, PCs, desktop tools, etc.)

❑ Configuring PCs

❑ Installing the front-end access tool

❑ Creating starter queries and reports

❑ Training for end-users, power users, strategic users, and operational users

❑ Developing a user support structure

DEPLOYMENT AND OPERATION
Deployment

Before a data warehouse can be rolled out, a support infrastructure needs to be in place and the end-users must be adequately trained. The level and depth of training varies as the skill levels of the users can vary considerably. Casual users, who typically run canned reports or create simple reports, can be trained with minimal training. However, heavy duty users, such as business analysts and power users, need more in-depth training as their requirements and dependency on the data warehouse is considerably higher.

Operating the data warehouse

After the data warehouse becomes operational, the data management process including extraction, transformation, staging, and load scheduling is automated wherever possible. The loading is scheduled based on one of two common procedures: bulk download (which refreshes the entire database periodically) and change-based replication (which copies the differences in data residing on different servers).

Once a data warehouse is up and running, it will continue to require attention in different ways. A successful data warehouse will see the numbers of users rise considerably, which can affect its performance—if it has not been properly sized. Also, support and enhancement requests will roll in. Some other common issues that need to be dealt with while operating a data warehouse include:

❑ Loading new data on a regular basis, which can range from real-time to weekly

❑ Ensuring uptime and reliability

❑ Managing the front-end tools

❑ Managing the back end components

❑ Updating data to reflect organizational changes, mergers and acquisitions, etc.

Chapter 12

Failure Causes and Common Mistakes

There are a number of reasons that have caused data warehouse project to fail or fall short of expectations. While each data warehouse implementation is unique, that is defined by its own set of variables, a number of common factors and mistakes have been identified and associated with the failure of such projects, which are explained in the following sections.

PLANNING AND APPROACH
Strategic planning is lacking

Many data warehouse projects are implemented without proper planning and consideration of its strategic importance to the organization. They are undertaken without the realization that a data warehouse project is different than an application development project which, consequently, leads to many unpleasant surprises. In many cases, data marts are designed and created without considering the possibility that they may be integrated into an enterprise data warehouse architecture in the future.

Approach is over-ambitious

When an organization implements its first data warehouse, it typically does not have experienced data warehouse professionals on its staff. Therefore, the risk of making serious mistakes is fairly high. However, despite lack of experience, many companies have implemented enterprise-wide data warehouse projects without first gaining experience through a pilot or data mart project.

Such an ambitious approach, without experienced staff to guide it, has often led to cost overruns, delays, and project failures.

Evaluation is lacking or flawed

A data warehouse system should not be implemented unless it is preceded by a thorough evaluation of the company's business, reporting and analytical requirements, as well as existing systems—transaction and reporting. The potential impact of the new system, and how it will integrate with or replace the organization's other applications, should be carefully studied before a decision is made to implement a data warehouse.

Focus is on technology

Some companies focus too much on technology because they are driven by the desire to be at the bleeding edge of hardware and software. Consequently, they focus on the technology—not the business and its requirements. This happens frequently when a data warehouse project is driven by the IT department, which tends to pay too much attention to the technology rather than the business needs of the organization.

Approach is casual

Many projects are approached with two misconceptions. First, that the data warehouse project is just another technical or database/application project. This is a fundamentally incorrect view because it is a business project—not a technical project. Second, a belief that a "how-to" or "do-it-yourself" book, or attending a data warehouse course, can prepare someone for implementing a data warehouse project.

Implementation barriers are not identified

A number of barriers can negatively impact the implementation of a data warehouse project. They include resistance from senior executives fearing loss of control, fallout resulting from lower level staff empowerment, functional process owners not being on board, hidden political agendas, departments having their own decision support systems, bad relationship with IT, inadequate funding, etc. The implementation barriers must be identified, at an early stage, in order to minimize the potential of their derailing the project. However, in many cases, this important task is not carried out and, consequently, project risk is increased.

Organization is not ready

An organization must be ready before it implements a data warehouse project. For such a project to succeed, it must have the support of three key groups: management, those affected by the implementation, as well as those implementing it. A data warehouse should not be implemented unless key personnel are behind the project and the organization is ready to accept change across the enterprise. In case the organization is not ready, it is advisable to delay the project until a higher level of support is available, which will increase the probability of success.

Procedures are deficient

Procedural factors often play a part in the failure of data warehouse projects. They include poor or deficient implementation and deployment, lack of formal process for involving users, undefined process for upgrading pilot or small-scale data marts into an enterprise data warehouse, absence of scope control mechanism, inadequate testing procedure, etc.

LEADERSHIP AND POLITICS
Wrong sponsorship

A data warehouse project must be sponsored by a senior functional executive who should have a vested in the project and its success. He should be powerful, respected, and decisive. The sponsor should be flexible, not be enamored by technology, and be user-oriented rather than technology-oriented. The sponsor should be able to obtain resources when required, encourage team work, motivate, and provide direction. A common mistake is to choose a sponsor who does not meet these basic characteristics.

Management is not on board

Many data warehouse projects, which demand a high level of commitment, have failed to meet expectations due to lack of management support at various stages of the project. When support is lacking or denied, the project can face serious problems due to funding issues, conflicts, failure to get adequate and appropriate resources, inability to resolve a wide range of issues requiring timely management intervention, etc.

Expectations are not well managed

In order to sell a data warehouse project, management expectations need to be raised. However, in some cases, such expectations are raised to unrealistically high levels, which can be a serious issue when they are not met. It is imperative that expectations be set very carefully, which is a very difficult task. If the expectations are not reasonably high, the project runs the risk of not being approved or its preferred resources may be allocated to a competing project. If the expectations are too high, and they are not subsequently met, the project will be considered a failure.

Desire to control supercedes business needs

Data warehouse projects can be quite political as a number of organizations and departments, with different priorities and agendas, can be involved in its implementation. Many department heads fear loss of control and, therefore, are reluctant to let others encroach on their turfs or provide needed buy-in. Frequently, there is conflict between functional users and IT, which views it as a technology project and does not favor the empowerment of business users.

Wrong communications

A common justification for a data warehouse project is that it helps executive decision making at all levels within the organization. While this is true, it must be communicated with care or problems can arise. For example, justifying the project by naively saying that the data warehouse will help managers make better decisions, which implies that they are poor decision makers, can backfire and antagonize key executives.

Project is political

A number of factors make data warehouse projects very political. They cause organizational and departmental boundaries to be crossed, open access to previously restricted data, empower those who had been denied access to valuable information, sometimes reengineer processes, and impact the way work is performed by many groups. Socio-technical factors, people and politics, which are relatively unimportant in conventional IT projects, are very important in data warehousing projects. In such projects, new rules exist and business users have more power. They need to be closely consulted during the design phase as well as the subsequent implementation and deployment phases.

DESIGN AND TECHNICAL FACTORS
Poor architecture

Many data warehouse projects fail because the system is built upon a poorly designed architecture. This can be manifested in a number of ways such as deficient schema, data access method, network architecture, client/server architecture, and inadequate metadata. Creating a data warehouse based on a flawed architecture is a very serious mistake because it is the most difficult, and costly, to rectify once it has been implemented. Hence, it is imperative that a top-notch data warehouse architect be used for designing the architecture.

Poor infrastructure planning

Inadequate infrastructure planning has led to many post-implementation issues such as performance, capacity, and scalability. It is common for well-designed and successful data warehouses to start having problems due to net-work overload and capacity problems shortly after becoming operational. The reason is that a successful data warehouse quickly draws more and more users, which can overwhelm it if the infrastructure is not designed to accommodate a quick and dramatic rise in usage. When demand soars, it affects both hardware and software requirements. This has caught many organizations by surprise and, consequently, forced them to make unplanned hardware and software expenditures.

Database upgrade strategy is flawed

The introduction of a new database system in an organization has many risks associated with it and requires a careful and measured approach. The upgrade of the OLTP system from a legacy non-relational database to a relational database, which is a complex undertaking, should not coincide with the implementation of a data warehouse. The introduction of relational database technology, if required for both the OLTP and data warehouse systems, should be phased—not simultaneous.

Inadequate components

The inadequacy of data warehouse components can lead to serious problems and, in extreme cases, project failure. The selected components can be inadequate or inappropriate for the particular project. There are many reasons for this problem including incorrect selection criteria, accepting vendor claims at face value, inadequate testing, limited scalability, improper sizing, lack of network traffic analysis, incorrect data volume estimate, incompatibility between components, etc.

Not differentiating between a database and a data warehouse

A fairly common mistake made by those implementing their first data warehouse project is their flawed assumption that a data warehouse is just like an OLTP database. Since they are unaware of the fundamental design difference between a traditional database and a data warehouse, normalization versus denormalization, they incorrectly assume that a conventional database system has to be designed—a relatively simple task that can be performed by many experienced in-house IT personnel. However, many do not realize until it is too late that a data warehouse is a process, encompassing many components, whose successful implementation requires knowledge of both business and technology.

Consensus regarding data definitions is lacking

Users must have confidence in the data warehouse data that they access and analyze. If there are any inconsistent results, it can cause loss of confidence and, consequently, make the warehouse less likely to be used. A common problem causing inconsistencies is the delivery of data with definitions that are overlapping and confusing. For example, a definition of revenue could be "total revenues minus returns", while another definition might be limited to "gross revenue." Unless such definitions are clear, queries will return results that are inconsistent and, consequently, lead to decision making mistakes.

Inadequate or too much data

Importing insufficient data into the data warehouse can limit the analysis that can be performed. Since highly granular data allows maximum analytical versatility, import of transaction data should be maximized even though it significantly increases data volumes. In general, the usefulness and versatility of a data warehouse increases as the data stored in it increases. However, storing too much data, especially if it is irrelevant, can have a negative impact because it can require extra effort for the ETL task, which can potentially delay the project. Therefore, the amount and type of data to be selected for import should be limited to whatever is required to make the users effective and efficient.

External data is ignored

It is a mistake to use summarized data as the foundation of a data warehouse because, in many cases, real value is to be found in the detailed transaction data. To maximize the benefits of a data warehouse, all potential data sources, external and internal, should be exploited. External data can be very useful and should not be ignored.

Wrong tools are selected

The selection of inappropriate tools can create many issues during implementation as well as ongoing operations. A company the author worked for bought a $600,000 ETL tool which was ultimately found to be inadequate. Consequently, custom code had to be written to perform the required ETL tasks. Many tools, while adequate in some environments, are incompatible with other tools used on a particular project. Consequently, all the tools and components should be selected very carefully.

IMPLEMENTATION AND DEPLOYMENT
Project goals are not clear

If the goals are unclear or inconsistent, it can spell trouble for the project. In the worst cases, where the deliverables are not specified and controls are lacking, the project can run into many serious problems due to ambiguous objectives, scope creep, disagreements over functionality, responsibilities, implementation issues, etc.

Inadequate project plan and inaccurate estimates

A data warehouse project must always be implemented according to a realistic project plan. Without such a tool, a project cannot be monitored and controlled effectively. A project is doomed to failure if the costs for various systems, and the time required to implement various activities, are not accurately estimated. A project that is estimated inaccurately will usually fail due to cost overruns and schedule slippage.

Scope creep

Scope creep, which is the bane of every IT project, frequently afflicts data warehouse projects. Scope must be controlled very tightly at every project stage. However, despite the best effort exerted by project management, scope does increase frequently. The key is to minimize scope creep if it cannot be eliminated completely. If scope is not carefully managed and controlled, risk will increase and the project will either exceed its budget or be delayed.

Inadequate testing and validation

Inadequate testing and validation can cause problems in two ways. First, due to loading failures, the ETL effort will require additional work which can potentially impact the cost and schedule. Second, if the data being imported into the data warehouse is not cleansed and validated, it can lead to various issues associated with the lack of data integrity. For example, queries will generate incorrect results and, consequently, lead to loss of confidence among users. If data warehouse users do not have confidence in its data, they will be reluctant to use it.

Lack of adequate attention to deployment

The design and construction phases receive the maximum attention during a data warehouse implementation project. However, the actual deployment does not get the attention it deserves, in some cases, even though it is an important and challenging task. When deployment problems arise, they can lead to the perception that the project is less than successful despite running very smoothly during the earlier phases. In extreme cases, it can cause the data warehouse to be viewed very negatively by the users and, consequently, create an acceptance issue.

Operation issues are not addressed adequately

The operation issues that do not get the attention they deserve include managing users (who can number in the thousands), data ownership, scheduling of data updates, change management, process for approvals, warehouse usage measurement for billing and charge back, tuning required for optimal performance, monitoring processing times for queries, etc.

Shortage of skilled data warehouse resources

Data warehousing has evolved and matured in the past decade—from an unproven to an established mainstream technology. However, while the professionals required to implement data warehouse projects are available in large numbers at this time, it is still difficult to find key resources who really understand data warehousing. In particular, there is a shortage of data warehouse architects, or designers, who can translate an organization's business requirements into a technical architecture that can be implemented efficiently and optimally.

Inadequate resources planned for data cleanup and validation

A considerable amount of effort is required to clean source data before it is introduced into the data warehouse. If this task is neglected, it can create many data migration problems during the implementation phase. It can also cause serious operational problems, after the data warehouse goes live, because queries can produce inconsistent and unreliable results due to the incorrect data.

Not realizing that data warehouse projects rarely end

The belief that problems will end once a data warehouse project is up and running is misplaced. After a data warehouse goes live, users continue to ask for enhancements, custom or additional reports, additional data, etc. Operational problems can encompass issues such as performance degradation, security, disaster recovery, backups, managing changes/additions in sources feeding the warehouse, user management, and other support issues.

REPORTING
Users cannot perform ad hoc reporting

The availability of powerful front-end access tools has been an important driver for the popularity of data warehousing. However, while power users have successfully mined data warehouses, end-users have not used the reporting tools to their full potential. Most of them limit their usage to executing starter pre-defined queries and reports provided to them. However, in a dynamic business environment, changes occur all the time. Therefore, when such users are unable to modify even simple reports, they are forced to seek IT help. However, creating or modifying simple reports is not the optimal use of highly skilled IT resources.

Decision support gets inadequate attention

When usage is primarily limited to ad hoc queries and simple reports, while decision support and analysis are neglected, it means that a very important data warehouse objective is being given insufficient attention. It should be realized that the maximum benefit, the biggest bang for the buck, is typically obtained through strategic analysis of data warehouse data. Data mining, slicing and dicing, and in-depth analysis can produce results that can pay for the data warehouse many times over.

Inappropriate data access tools

The choice of the front-end tool for accessing data warehouse data can have far reaching implications. If the front-end tool is not accepted by the users, the data warehouse will either fail or not be able to achieve any measurable success. Hence, the data access tool, which must be intuitive and user-friendly, must be selected carefully. While a number of factors need to be considered such as cost, performance, and security, the most important factor is its ability to meet the needs of the users.

Chapter 13

Guidelines, Tips, and Trends

PLANNING
Prepare a strategic plan

The foundation of a data warehouse implementation should be the organization's strategic plan which should specify the mission, purpose, objectives, and goals along with the strategy for achieving them. Such a tool is management's roadmap and guide for helping the organization achieve its objectives.

Determine strategic business requirements

The strategic business and information requirements must be determined before any data warehouse is built. Without these requirements in place, which can be derived from the strategic plan and its performance measures, the basis for the enterprise information and data warehouse architectures will be missing. The establishment of performance measures help management determine if there is progress in meeting its goals and objectives.

Plan for the enterprise

Many data marts are planned and implemented without enterprise considerations. The data marts, in many cases, ultimately rollup into a corporate data warehouse. They are designed by semi-experts and, often, do not incorporate any planning for ultimately merging them into an enterprise data warehouse infrastructure. This deficiency ultimately leads to a less than optimal data warehouse solution from both a technical and financial perspective.

Realize that data warehouse requirements can be different

Each data warehouse implementation is unique. The business, systems, data sources, architecture, environment, components, project staff and skills, constraints, etc. can be different. Hence, do not view all data warehouse projects as being the same or that one size fits all. Consider the unique requirements and proceed accordingly.

Identify areas that can help achieve corporate goals

An enterprise data warehouse will never provide the same level of benefits in different functional areas. Therefore, the areas or processes that can help achieve the organization's strategic long-term goals should be implemented first. Identify the business areas which can benefit the most from a data warehouse implementation. Typically, these include sales, customers, marketing, and products. The list of important subject areas should be prioritized and the top ones should be implemented first.

Clearly specify objectives and goals

The project goals and objectives should be clearly specified, which will ensure that there are no unrealistic expectations. Clearly defined objectives and requirements will ensure that the scope, and consequently the project, will not be risked due to ambiguities and misplaced expectations.

Get the right resources

The success of a data warehouse project depends on the availability of the required resources. The project implementation team should include the right mix of functional and technical personnel. The important positions should be staffed by functional experts who understand the business and information needs of the organization. While consultants should be used, as they can be very valuable, excessive use of such resources should be avoided as it limits knowledge transfer.

Select partners carefully

Many organizations embarking on a data warehouse project do not have personnel with data warehousing skills. Therefore, they are forced to use implementation partners. The consulting partners must be reliable and competent. They must be selected very carefully through a well-established screening and evaluation process. Failure to select the right implementation partner can be a very costly mistake.

Do not favor technology over business

A data warehouse project is a business project rather than a technology project. Its objective should be to provide easily accessible data and information, rather than implementing state-of-the-art technology. It is a mistake to believe that technology will solve all problems. Technology, instead of being viewed as the solution, should be used only as an enabler.

USER-CENTRIC APPROACH
Appreciate the impact on users and managers

An enterprise data warehouse project is a huge project that touches an organization's most important functional areas. Its impact is similar to a re-engineering project and its success or failure can have far reaching implications. A data warehouse suddenly empowers users and surprises entrenched managers, who find themselves in a less controlling position. Therefore, an attempt should be made to understand and appreciate the impact, on both people and processes, of introducing a data warehouse into the organization.

Analyze end-user business requirements

Many data warehouse projects have failed because they focused on integrating and supplying data to the warehouse, rather than understanding user needs and requirements. It is imperative that user requirements be carefully analyzed, and met, if the warehouse is to be heavily utilized and be successful. A determination must be made regarding the reports and queries the users will need to generate. Additionally, the type of decision making that needs to be supported must be determined as it will influence the selection of the front-end access tool.

Analyze end-user tool requirements

The data access front-end tool should be selected with the end-users in mind. The tool, whose primary selection criteria is ease of use, should satisfy end-user needs and not stretch the ability of common users to use it. The end-users, who are often non-technical, should be provided a tool that interfaces with them in business terms, rather than cryptic technical jargon. Such a tool should be flexible and allow ad hoc querying by unsophisticated users. It must not require heavy usage of IT resources for the creation of reports and queries.

Make end-users happy

A data warehouse needs to be sold to business executives and end-users. To achieve such an objective, they should be involved as early as possible and the project should be presented as a joint venture between the implementers and users. Before a front-end tool is selected, input from all types of users should be elicited and evaluated. During the design and development stages, functional experts, data owners and users at various organizational levels must be involved. Such an approach will ensure easy acceptance.

Do not ignore training needs

Project team members, including functional and IT staff, as well as end-users must be provided with adequate and timely training. If end-users are not well-trained, the level of acceptance of the system, and its utilization, can be compromised. Training should be tailored so that it meets the requirements of all data warehouse users, whose skill levels can vary tremendously. The needs of most casual users, who typically run canned reports, differs considerably from those of power users and business analysts who mine the data warehouse in innovative ways.

LEADERSHIP AND POLITICS
Do not act arbitrarily

A data warehouse is a valuable enterprise resource that is useful to, and tapped by, a large number of users belonging to various divisions, departments, and functional areas. Their needs and requirements should be carefully determined during the planning and design phases of the data warehouse project. Acting arbitrarily and ignoring users can derail a project, cause finger pointing, and prevent the warehouse from becoming a valuable source of data for the ignored users.

Do not let IT be the project driver

The IT department should not drive a data warehouse implementation because it is a business—not a technology project. However, ignoring IT can be a problem because functional leaders do not always appreciate technical complexities and, hence, can become too demanding. A factor that can contribute significantly to the success of a data warehouse project is cooperation between the organization's IT department and its business/functional groups. The project manager, who should understand the business aspects and needs, must belong to the business/functional side of the organization—which has a greater stake in the success of the project.

Market project successes

Success breeds success. Therefore, implementation successes should be publicized. Wherever possible, measurable successes, as indicated by various performance metrics, should be publicized. If a data mart is successful, it can bring more business units on board once they become aware of its benefits and the in-house implementation success.

Anticipate political issues

A data warehouse project is political in nature due to the large number of departments and stakeholders involved with it, cross-currents, conflicting priorities and requirements, and other factors. Therefore, it is important that political issues be anticipated because they can impact the project negatively by creating conflicts, delaying decisions, preventing buy-in, etc. The project leader must be politically savvy and know how to deal with issues in such an environment.

Obtain management commitment

A data warehouse project can lead to many changes, which can range from minor to significant, within an organization. These changes can impact the way business is run in some areas. If the changes introduced by the data warehouse are to be accepted, management must be on board. If it is perceived that management is not behind the project, the resistance can be significant. The project sponsor must be strong and have a vested stake in the project.

DESIGN AND TECHNICAL FACTORS
Understand difference between operational and DSS requirements

Many people who implement data warehouse projects, including IT and business personnel, are not even aware of basic data warehousing concepts. They incorrectly assume that a data warehouse is just a large database. They do not realize that there are fundamental differences in the requirements and needs pertaining to conventional operational reporting, ad hoc querying, and decision support applications.

Evaluate development approach and methodology

A data warehouse should be implemented using a well-established methodology. The development approach and potential implementation methodologies should be evaluated prior to project implementation. Every data warehouse implementation is unique and various development approaches can be used, such as top-down or bottom-up. No project should be implemented without a structured approach or a proven methodology.

Do not prematurely narrow down the solutions

Numerous choices are available for designing the infrastructure and selecting the components required for a data warehousing solution. A mistake made by some organizations is to narrow the range of solutions before understanding the problem and its environment. Such an approach limits the implementation of an optimal solution for the organization's information needs.

Realize that business rules can be conflicting

The various groups using a data warehouse can have conflicting business rules that can impact the selection, screening, and import of data from various sources. If the definitions used by different groups are inconsistent, the results of calculations can vary, which can create many issues. For example, using different definitions, the net sales figure can vary depending on whether returns are included or excluded. If such potential issues are not addressed and resolved before the data warehouse is put into operation, the conflicting results can undermine its credibility.

Plan a solid architecture

The data warehouse must be designed within the context of the enterprise information architecture, which is based on the organization's information requirements that support the strategic enterprise requirements. The foundation of the enterprise information architecture is the enterprise data architecture (which is a fully normalized enterprise data model) and the enterprise technical architecture (which lays out the infrastructure, platforms, hardware, operating systems, etc.).

Make business requirements the architecture's foundation

The business requirements of the enterprise should be reflected in the data warehouse design and architecture. Business requirements, not specific technologies, should be the basis for the enterprise data model and components. The architecture should reflect the need for analytical processing rather than transaction processing, a distinction that is missed in many instances. The chosen data warehouse architecture must be well understood by the implementation team.

Design a scalable architecture

A data warehouse must be scaleable and flexible, which will prevent it being a victim of its own success. Success causes data warehouse usage to rise tremendously, which leads to issues if the infrastructure is unable to scale adequately. Due to the explosive growth in the generation and storage of data, scalability has become a very important design factor that cannot be ignored.

Do not underestimate migration difficulties

A widespread problem is underestimating the effort and difficulties associated with migrating data from multiple sources into the integrated data warehouse. Often, the quality of data is far worse than expected, which can cause many problems and delay a critical task—validating the data being imported. It is advisable not to have unrealistic data quality expectations. Be prepared to find very dirty data.

Do not underestimate ETL effort

One of the most difficult tasks, which is also the most costly, is extracting, transforming, and loading data from multiple sources into the data warehouse. This task is conducted over a long period and is often underestimated. Any shortcut in the ETL process impacts data warehouse integrity and, therefore, must be avoided.

Do not ignore historical data

The more data a data warehouse contains, both historical and operational, the more useful it can be to those mining it. It is difficult and, in some cases, impossible to determine any meaningful trend if the data period is short. Determining trends over time, especially for strategic purposes, is easier if the analysis period is longer. Therefore, load as much relevant historical data as can be accommodated in the data warehouse.

IMPLEMENTATION AND DEPLOYMENT
Identify factors that can impact implementation

Many factors can derail the implementation of a data warehouse or its deployment. The potential roadblocks should be identified, early on in the project, so that appropriate and timely action can be taken to minimize or eliminate them. If this task is not performed, it will increase the risk significantly and force the project team to be reactive, rather than proactive.

Favor best practices

A data warehouse project is a complex and risky undertaking. It should be implemented using best practices and techniques, which can reduce risk and improve the odds of executing a successful implementation on time and within budget. Use a proven full life-cycle development methodology.

Start with a pilot

There are many advantages of starting with a pilot data warehouse project. Such a project requires a smaller budget, short implementation time, can be limited to a small department or a single subject, is less risky, and provides valuable experience to the implementation team. If the pilot project fails, its impact will be limited to a small group and the overall enterprise data warehouse plan will not be derailed.

Implement using a project plan

A data warehouse project should be managed, implemented, and deployed using a detailed project plan that is based on a realistic schedule. While this may appear to be standard practice for a development project, the fact is that many data warehouse projects have been implemented without a formal project plan. With no monitoring and control mechanism in place, such projects, not surprisingly, have failed.

Specify responsibilities and deliverables

The project responsibilities should be clearly specified. Wherever possible, specific project tasks with corresponding responsibilities should be assigned to individual team members. The deliverables for each phase and important project milestones, with responsibilities, should be specified. The responsibilities of a consulting partner working on the project should also be clearly specified.

Select a motivated project team

The project team members should be drawn from the various functional departments as well as IT. The functional experts should be decision makers who are highly motivated and able to work in a team environment. They should have strategic vision and good analytical skills. The team members, who must be fully dedicated to the project, must have the appropriate skills, knowledge, and experience if they are to make a meaningful contribution to the project.

Choose an experienced leader for the project

The project leader must be experienced in implementing data warehouse projects and should have a good understanding of business as well as technology. He should have excellent project management skills, which is a fundamental requirement for the project manager position, and closely manage and control the project. Ideally, the project manager should be familiar with the various data warehouse components and tools.

Control the scope

The inability to keep scope under control can pose a serious risk for the project from both the cost and schedule perspective. Therefore, a serious effort should be made to control scope creep at every stage of the project. Care should be taken that small innocuous requests and minor enhancements are not implemented if they fall outside the defined scope because they can quickly get out of hand.

Manage rollout

Even a successful implementation can lose its luster due to a rollout that is not well-planned and received. The data warehouse rollout should be planned in detail. If possible, the rollout to a very large number of users should be carried out in phases. Such an approach reduces training and support issues. It also enables any production issues to be handled easily and effectively.

DATA WAREHOUSING TRENDS
Faster and more powerful hardware

As data warehouses have grown bigger and bigger, the hardware required to support them has grown faster and more powerful. With terabyte data warehouses fairly common now, analyzing such huge databases will require greater usage of, and reliance on, high speed hardware such as massively parallel processors (MPP), which can speed up query processing, data loading, creating indexes, etc.

Integration of databases with analytical tools

It is expected that proprietary OLAP database servers will continue to become more powerful. Vendors of relational databases will enhance their products to offer greater support for data warehousing requirements. They will integrate OLAP functionality into their core products, support multi-dimensional tools, and become more flexible in their objective of supporting decision support applications.

Integration with transaction systems

The ETL task seriously challenges every data warehouse implementation team. In order to minimize the difficulties associated with this task, vendors will make a serious attempt to integrate the data warehouse with the source transaction databases. Their success in this area will enable the extraction, transformation, and loading routines to be simpler, less prone to errors, and considerably faster.

Integration across tools and platforms

The quest for data that can be used for decision support extends to all parts of the enterprise as well as external systems. It is expected that there will be a continued push towards integrating the data warehouse across the plethora of available tools, platforms, and sources in order to make it even more useful. Vendors will build alliances or develop products that will enable tighter integration from end-to-end. Business intelligence software will continue to improve and offer features such as workflow and collaboration.

Integration with ERP and CRM systems

ERP and CRM systems generate and store huge amounts of data that can feed into a data warehouse. It is expected that they will be very closely integrated so that the data transfer between them is fast and seamless. Integration will enable analysis that, besides being faster, will encompass various applications and systems.

Scalability

The success of data warehousing technology, and the resulting explosion in the amount of data stored and the number of users, has made scalability an important issue. Scalability will remain on the front-burner for some time to come due to continued data warehousing growth and the need for improved performance.

Web-enabled access

The trend towards thin clients and remote access will continue. By enabling web access, no code will need to be installed on the desktop, which will considerably reduce IT support. Enabling web access to the data warehouse will have two benefits: provide remote analysis capabilities and also enable data in the target database to be refreshed through the web. It is expected that bundled products such as web servers, access tools, and databases will be widely available.

Improved query and analysis tools

The trend towards more intuitive and powerful analytical tools will continue unabated. Multi-dimensional tools will become more powerful. Considerable attention will be paid to analysis tools, especially OLAP and data mining, and integrating them with the data warehouse database. No single tool will meet all the requirements of an enterprise because users have varying skills, which range from casual to sophisticated, and their needs can range from simple reporting to slicing and dicing. Most of the front-end access tools will be web-enabled. Their functionality will enable them to cross subject data marts and also access heterogeneous data sources on different platforms.

Unstructured data

Historically, structured data has been primarily used to populate data ware-houses. However, the demands for innovative analysis and ability to access unstructured data will be the impetus for data warehouses to be populated with unstructured data such as text, images, etc. They will be able to handle unstructured data and have the ability to add and search such data.

Merge capabilities

Data warehouses will be provided the capability to merge data from different sources. This technique, known as fusion, is still in its infancy. However, with research underway in what can be a significant cost-saving technique, it is expected to become widely available in the not too distant future.

Agent technology

Typically, a data warehouse is analyzed and the results obtained are used to take some action(s). For this procedure, an analyst has to spend considerable time and effort to reach the point where some exceptions are noted. With agent technology, the system itself can provide alerts based on exceptions within the data stored in the warehouse. The benefits from this technology are very appealing and, hence, we can expect its application and usage to grow.

Visualization

Visualization enables data to be presented graphically in charts and diagrams. Using this technique, transaction data or summary information can be converted into graphs and charts. It is expected that data warehouse visualization will be widely used for supporting interaction, trend analysis, as well as performing charting and drill-down.

Appendix

List of Data Warehousing Vendors

Data Integration
Data quality and cleansing

Acxiom

AMB Dataminers

Arkidata

Ascential Software

Avellino Technologies

Computer Associates

Corworks

Data Instrument Group

Datactics

DataFlux

DataMentors

Datanomics

EnableSoft

Evoke Software

Experian

Firstlogic

Group 1 Software

Innovative Systems

Incon Solutions

Kronus Software

Melissa Data

Metagenix

Odeyssey SA

Optima Database Management

Oracle

Pitney Bowes

Sagent technology

SAS Institute

Search Software America

Similarity Systems

SQL Power Group

Trillium Software

Mapping and transformation

Ab Initio Software
Ascential Software
Business Objects
Coglin Mill
Cognos
Computer Associates
CoSORT/IRI
Data Habitat
Data Mirror
Decision Support
Embarcadero Technology
Evolutionary Technologies
Hummingbird
IBM

Informatica
ISoft
IWay Software (Information Builders)
Microsoft
Oracle
Paladyne
Reveleus
Sagent Technology
SAP AG
Sapior
SAS Institute
Solonde
SQL Power Group
Sybase

Metadata management

Allen Systems Group
Ascential Software
Computer Associates
Data Advantage Group
Hummingbird
IBM
Informatica
Information Builders

MetaMatrix
Microsoft
Oracle
SAS Institute
Soft Experience
Sybase
Techquila
Unicorn Solutions

Data movement

Accelerant Software
Alebra technologies
Ascential Software
BMC Software
CDB Software
Computer Associates
Corworks

CrossAccess
DataMirror
E-zdata.net
HiT Software
Informatica
Information Transport Associates
Insession Technologies

Ispirer Systems
Lakeview Technology
Legato Systems
Princeton Softech
Quest Software
SAS Institute

Strategic Product Integration
Striva
Syncsort
TeleMagic
Teradata
Vision Solutions

Data conversion

CipherSoft
Computer Associates
Data Junction

DataMirror
Information Builders
IWay Software (Information Builders)

Data access

Allen Systems Group
Attunity
Computer Associates
CrossAccess
HiT Software
Hummingbird
IBM
Idera
Informatica

IWay Software (Information Builders)
Mercator Software
MetaMatrix
QED Business Systems
Raining Data
SAS Institute
Simba Technologies
Unisys

Data Warehouse Design
Data modeling and analysis

Aleri
Computer Associates
Embarcadero Technologies
MEGA International
Oracle
Popkin Software

Quest Software
Sagent Technology
Stirling Systems Group
Sybase
Visible Systems

Data warehousing toolsets

Aruna
DataHabitat
IBM
IT-Map
Kalido
Magma Solutions
New Generation Software
Oracle

PeopleSOft
Reveleus
Sagent technology
SAP AG
SAS Institute
SQL Power group
Sybase

Infrastructure
Database management systems

Computer Associates
IBM
Microsoft
MySQL AB
NCR

Netezza
Oracle
Sybase
Teradata

Multi-dimensional databases

Applix
Comshare
Crystal Decisions
Dinesional Insight
Gentia Software
Hyperion
Information Builders
IBM

Microsoft
MIS
Oracle
Pilot Software
SAS Institute
Seagate Software
SPSS
WhiteLight Systems

Data accelerators

Ab Initio Software
Appfluent Technology
Aruna
Ascential
CoSORT/IRI
Data Assurance Technology Associates

Dynamic Information Systems
InterSystems
MaxScan
OSE Systems
TimesTen

Storage management systems

Brocade Communications Systems
CommVault Systems
Compaq Computer
Corworks
DataCore Software
Dell Computer
EMC
FileTek
Hewlett-Packard
Hitachi Data Systems
IBM

Legato Systems
LSI Logic
McData
Network Appliance
Overland Storage
Qlogic
Storage Area Solutions
Storage Technology
Stratus Technologies
Sun Microsystems
Veritas Software

Servers

Compaq Computer
Dell Computer
Hewlett-Packard
IBM

Netezza
Stratus Technologies
Sun Microsystems
Vecmar Computer Solutions

Analysis
Query and reporting

Addinsoft
Arcplan
Aruna
Auguri
Brio Technology
Business Objects
Cognos
Computer Associates
CorVu
Crystal Decisions
Databeacon
Decision Support
Dimensional Insight
Dimensional Strategies
Hummingbird
Hyperion

IlumifiAPF
Meta5
MicroStrategy
New Generation Software
Noetix
Oracle
Panorama Software Systems
Qualitech Solutions
Relational Solutions
Renegade Software
Speedware
StayinFront
Sybase
Systrack
TARGIT
XL Cubed

OLAP

Accrue Software
Allen Systems Group
AlphaBlox
Applix
Arcplan
Brio Technology
Business Objects
Clarity Systems
Cognos
Computer Associates
Comshare
CorVu
Crystal Decisions
Data Beacon
Data Dynamics
Dimensional Insight
Flintfox
Gentia Software
Hummingbird
Hyperion
IBM
Ideasoft
Information Builders
Microsoft
MicroStrategy
MIS
Oracle
Panorama Software Systems
Paristech
Pilot Software
ProClarity
Sagent Technology
SAS
Speedware
Sybase
Temtec International
Visual OLAP P/L
Walker
ZTI

Data mining

Angoss Software
Cognos
Computer Associates
Visual OLAP P/L
Data Mining Technologies
DB Miner Technology
Genalytics
Group 1 Software
IBM
Information Discovery
Insightful
Isoft
Magnify
Megaputer Intelligence
Microsoft
Molecular Mining
NCR
NeuralWare
Oracle
PolyVista
Salford Systems
Sand technology
SAS Institute
Sightward
Spotfire
SPSS
StatSoft
Teradata
Unica
WizSoft

Administration and operations
Database management

Babboo
BMC Software
Bradmark
CDB Software
Computer Associates
DGI
E-zdata.net
Embarcadero Technologies
Expand Beyond

Heroix
IBM
Insession Technologies
Krell Software
Oracle
Quest Software
Red Gate Software
Teradata
Xtivia Technologies

Index

0-595-29069-8

CPSIA information can be obtained
at www.ICGtesting.com
Printed in the USA
FFOW03n1040060216
21186FF